"Like a glass of water when you ~~~ dehydration, *One with My Lord* ~~~ you needed. In his distinctively inviting style, Sam Allberry helps us drink in one of the most vital and consistently taught truths of Scripture: that we are 'in Christ' and that this changes everything. I highly recommend that you read this book and take time to process what it means."

> **Rebecca McLaughlin**, author, *Confronting Jesus: 9 Encounters with the Hero of the Gospels*

"For too long the glory of the Christian's union with Christ has been overlooked, understated, and misunderstood. In this book, Sam Allberry has done a wonderful job of drawing our attention to the mystery and the majesty of this union. *One with My Lord* is a delight to read, an encouragement to our faith, and a witness to God's welcome of his children in Christ."

> **Kyle Worley**, Pastor, Mosaic Church, Richardson, Texas; Cohost, *Knowing Faith Podcast*

"Being 'in Christ,' Sam Allberry says, is 'the Bible's primary way of talking about what it means to be a follower of Jesus.' Allberry helps us see the wonder of salvation and the Christian life through the lens of union with Christ. In his delightfully clear and accessible style, he takes us through various aspects of what it means to be a man or woman 'in Christ.' This warmly pastoral work is grounded in careful reading of the Scriptures and serious theological reflection. Allberry shows us that union with Christ is richer, broader, and deeper than we might have imagined, with very practical implications for everyday life. Read this book and be encouraged."

> **Mark D. Thompson**, Principal, Moore Theological College

"Sam Allberry's writing is always refreshing and rooted in real experience, but this book really stands out. Allberry leads us gently through many different scriptures, not only to help us understand even the trickier passages but also to show how it all fits together. He clears up our misunderstandings, relates to our confusions and failures, and still makes it all about Jesus! *One with My Lord* is a vital and deeply pastoral book that helps us make more sense of both the Bible and our messy lives."

> **Mark Meynell**, Director (Europe and Caribbean), Langham Preaching; writer; preacher; cultural apologist

One with My Lord

Other Crossway Books by Sam Allberry

7 Myths about Singleness

What God Has to Say about Our Bodies: How the Gospel Is Good News for Our Physical Selves

You're Not Crazy: Gospel Sanity for Weary Churches (coauthored with Ray Ortlund)

One with My Lord

The Life-Changing Reality of Being in Christ

Sam Allberry

WHEATON, ILLINOIS

One with My Lord: The Life-Changing Reality of Being in Christ

© 2024 by Sam Allberry

Published by Crossway
      1300 Crescent Street
      Wheaton, Illinois 60187

Parts of chapter 3 are adapted from Sam Allberry, "Original Sin Can Make Us Compassionate," Desiring God, August 27, 2022, https://www.desiringGod.org/. Used by permission.

Parts of chapter 5 are adapted from Sam Allberry, "When You Feel Like a (Christian) Imposter," The Gospel Coalition, October 27, 2018, https://www.thegospelcoalition.org/. Used by permission.

Published in association with the literary agency of Wolgemuth & Associates.

Cover design: Matt Lehman

First printing 2024

Printed in the United States of America

Trade paperback ISBN: 978-1-4335-8915-7
ePub ISBN: 978-1-4335-8918-8
PDF ISBN: 978-1-4335-8916-4

Library of Congress Cataloging-in-Publication Data

Names: Allberry, Sam, author.
Title: One with my Lord : the life-changing reality of being in Christ / Sam Allberry.
Description: Wheaton, Illinois : Crossway, 2024. | Includes bibliographical references and indexes.
Identifiers: LCCN 2023052628 (print) | LCCN 2023052629 (ebook) | ISBN 9781433589157 (trade
   paperback) | ISBN 9781433589164 (pdf) | ISBN 9781433589188 (epub)
Subjects: LCSH: Christian life—Biblical teaching. | Jesus Christ.
Classification: LCC BV4501.3 .A445 2024 (print) | LCC BV4501.3 (ebook) | DDC 248.4—dc23/
   eng/20240220
LC record available at https://lccn.loc.gov/2023052628
LC ebook record available at https://lccn.loc.gov/2023052629

Crossway is a publishing ministry of Good News Publishers.

VP   33   32   31   30   29   28   27   26   25   24
15   14   13   12   11   10   9   8   7   6   5   4   3   2   1

For Brian and Leslie Roe

"They refreshed my spirit."
1 Corinthians 16:18

Contents

Introduction

WHEN I LAST HAD any extended time watching daytime
TV—I was at home, sick—it became quickly apparent to me
that we have a fixation with properties. There were shows about
renovating homes, finding homes in the country or in the Caribbean, homes being auctioned, homes on a budget, homes of the
super wealthy. Even when we're not wanting or needing to move
to a new home, it can be instinctive to look up property prices.
When I'm on vacation, I'll often find out how much it would
cost to live there and wonder about what life would look like if
that was where I was based.

It is not hard to see why we're fixated on things like this. Many of
us have a deep sense that once we find the right home, everything
else will fall into place. Work will be more meaningful, time off
more peaceful, family life more fulfilling. For some it is all about
location—the right amount of bustle, the right amount of space. Or
maybe it's the environment—being up in the mountains or down
by the coast. Or maybe it's the house itself—whether its roomy
enough, cozy enough, old enough, or modern enough. Whatever
it is, once that's sorted out, life will finally start to flourish.

There is a sense in which this instinct is right. We're physical creatures. Having a sense of place, of belonging, matters. And the Bible says there *is* an environment in which we can truly flourish, somewhere we *will* truly feel we belong, where life *will* slot into place—somewhere that will feel deeply *right.*

But it is not a physical location. It doesn't have a zip code. You won't find it on your GPS app. And there's not an economic threshold you need to reach to even think about getting in on it. It's an entirely different kind of place.

Before I recently moved to the United States, I spent several years living in a British town called Maidenhead, which doesn't have much to distinguish it other than that its railway bridge has two of the widest brick spans in the world and that the neighboring town is Windsor. Windsor, of course, is the year-round home of the British monarch.

This proximity to Windsor made quite a difference. As local residents, we had free access to the castle any time it was open. You could even see it in the distance from just up the road from my house. But more than that, it meant we lived in the *Royal* Borough of Windsor and Maidenhead and in the *Royal* County of Berkshire.

But this is not the only royal place where we can find ourselves. As Christians, we find ourselves in an altogether perfect spiritual location: in *Christ* himself.

Being in Christ is the topic of this book because it is the heart-beat of the Christian faith. It is a way of understanding our relationship with Jesus that might be unfamiliar to us but that is reflected on virtually every page of any New Testament letter. It reminds us that as well as being our Savior, our Lord, our teacher, and our friend, Jesus is also—in a way—our home, our place, our location. And we, as well as being those who submit to him, worship him, follow him, and imitate him, are those who now find ourselves to be *in* him.

This, it turns out, is no minor detail. It is what helps us best understand how we relate to Christ, how we can receive all that he has done for us, how we can move forward confidently with him, and how we find ourselves now deeply bound up with others also seeking to do the same. It is what makes the Christian life make the most sense. It is all these things because it is the Bible's primary way of talking about what it means to be a follower of Jesus. And once we're clear on that, we can be much clearer on *him*. It is, simply, the only place to be.

1

Found in Christ

. . . in order that I may gain Christ and be found in him.

PHILIPPIANS 3:8–9

I CAN PINPOINT the exact moment I finally had to admit I was middle aged. I was traveling through London and needed to make a quick connection at Paddington Station. The plan was to bound up the stairs from the underground station, glance quickly at the main departures board to check the platform of my connection, and get to the train just in time to board before it left—and to do all this without having to break my stride. In reality, I did bound up the stairs from the underground. I did glance at the departures board. And then I stopped.

I couldn't read any of the information on the board. It was a digital display. All the characters had a blurry halo; I could make out the individual letters and numbers only by walking right up to the board and squinting hard at it. (Amazingly, I made my connection—if barely.) For years I had prided myself on having great eyesight. Now I knew I needed glasses.

But I hadn't realized just *how much* I needed them.

When I finally got them, I could see the departures board at Paddington Station. But what surprised me was just how clearly I could now see *everything else*. It was like the whole world was now in high definition. I could now see distant trees and buildings in crisp detail. Everything was now more focused, much clearer.

Spiritual Spectacles

I had a similar experience when I started reflecting on two words that occur together repeatedly in the New Testament—"in Christ." These words are used to describe the true reality of Christian believers. It is a doctrine theologians call *union with Christ*, the idea that when people come to faith in Jesus, they are united to him spiritually. They are not just followers of Christ; they are in some sense now situated *in* him.

This idea is key to understanding the heart of the Christian faith. It brings it all into much better focus. What had seemed to me somewhat blurry truths and concepts now had a sharper definition. The contours of the Christian landscape were easier to see. The connections between different parts of Christian truth were now more obvious and vital. I now had a clearer vision of things.

Lens seems to be the right word for thinking about it. I knew, at some level, that I had a relationship with Jesus and that this meant being deeply connected to him. I had seen the "in Christ" language and related expressions throughout the New Testament. But I had never thought to dwell on them and consider what they might mean. As I started to look at this concept, I found myself looking through it: seeing everything else through the lens of this truth. It changed my whole world.

When I first became a Christian, I was primarily thinking in terms of being a follower of Jesus. I knew he was my Lord and Savior. I knew he would do a far better job of running my life than I could. I knew that he had died for me and risen again, that I could trust him with my life. All that was true, gloriously so. But I didn't really understand how it all fit together. There was Christ, somewhere over there, and here was I, at a distance, wanting with all my heart to keep up with him. I knew who he was and what I was called to. I knew that somehow he would help me be a follower. But that's as far as I could understand it. Conceptually, it was as if Jesus was at the other end of the universe from me, and I was always going to struggle to follow him at such a distance.

A Preferred Designation

One of the surprises when we turn the pages of the New Testament is how little the word "Christian" comes up. Given that this is *the* book for Christians, you would expect it to be littered with references to Christians and Christianity.

In fact, the word "Christian" appears only three times, the first of which is as a nickname for these new followers of Jesus: "And in Antioch the disciples were first called Christians" (Acts 11:26). Many think this was initially intended to be demeaning, the equivalent of "little Christs" or "Christlings," but it evidently stuck and—whatever the intentions—clearly was no great embarrassment to Christians, as we've happily carried the label ever since.

But whereas the word "Christian" is used only three times in the New Testament, the language of being "in Christ" and related expressions (e.g., "in him") occur many dozens of times. Paul alone uses this terminology more than 160 times. You can open the Bible on the page of virtually every New Testament letter and see this language, often several times. This is the New Testament's default way of speaking of followers of Jesus. A few examples will show us how striking this pattern is.

At one point in his writing to the Corinthians, Paul describes an anonymous Christian man:

> I know a man in Christ who fourteen years ago was caught up to the third heaven—whether in the body or out of the body I do not know, God knows. And I know this man was caught up into paradise—whether in the body or out of the body I do not know, God knows—and he heard things that cannot be told, which man may not utter. (2 Cor. 12:2–4)

Paul is talking about a (so far) nameless Christian who has been given a unique spiritual experience. Paul is a little fuzzy on some of the details. This man saw something of "the third heaven," but Paul doesn't know if it was a vision or whether he was literally there in person. Twice he admits, "I do not know, God knows."

We might think that uncertainty understandable if this were someone else's experience and if Paul were only describing what he had heard secondhand. But Paul goes on to show that he has actually been talking about himself. He talks about "the surpassing greatness of the revelations" and how easily he might have become conceited by seeing them (2 Cor. 12:7). Paul had been given backstage access to parts of heaven no one else normally gets to see.

For various reasons, Paul has been reluctant to ever share about this experience, but circumstances have compelled him to. Opponents in Corinth are running a smear campaign against Paul, trying to turn the Corinthian church away from him. One of their arguments seems to be that they had an inside track with God, that they had experienced special visions and revelations from God. So Paul is trying to do two tricky things at once: (1) show his readers that such visions alone are not signs of spiritual maturity and authority and (2) demonstrate that he's not just saying this because he's never had any. This isn't a case of sour grapes. Paul is in the awkward position of having to explain that he actually *has* had visions and revelations—in fact, surpassing anything his opponents had experienced—while at the same time trying to show that this is not the sort of thing a Christian should boast in. The fact that this extraordinary revelation occurred fourteen years ago and that Paul has never once mentioned it until now shows that it has not been the focus of his ministry.

So in his awkward reluctance to bring this up, Paul initially talks about this experience using third-person language—"I know a man who had an amazing vision of heaven"—before spilling the beans that it was really him all along.

What is significant for us is the language Paul uses to do this. If it were us writing today, we would probably say something like "I know a Christian man who fourteen years ago . . ." But Paul says, "I know a man in Christ." That, to him, is the most natural and obvious way to talk about himself. And he's presuming it's the most natural and obvious way for his readers to understand it too. He doesn't have to include a sidebar explaining what "being in Christ" means. He just refers to "a man in Christ," and everyone knows exactly what he's talking about. It was the go-to terminology. On a census form, Paul presumably wouldn't put "Christian" but "a man in Christ." If it is so instinctive for Paul, and not so for us, it suggests that we are missing something significant about what it means to be a follower of Jesus.

"In Christ" in the New Testament

Another example comes in the book of Acts. Luke is describing the growth of the early church. They have already faced some significant obstacles: opposition from some of the local authorities insisting that Peter and John no longer preach to anyone in the name of Jesus (Acts 4:17), as well as the beginnings of problems within the Christian community, with Ananias and Sapphira judged by God for trying to deceive everyone about how much they had been giving to the Lord (Acts 5:9). Yet through it all, the apostles remained faithful. The whole church was gripped by a fear of God (Acts 5:11).

Luke then gives this summary of the progress of the ministry at that point:

> Now many signs and wonders were regularly done among the people by the hands of the apostles. And they were all together in Solomon's Portico. None of the rest dared join them, but the people held them in high esteem. And more than ever believers were added to the Lord, multitudes of both men and women. (Acts 5:12–14)

A lot is happening—preaching, signs and wonders, and various powerful, supernatural healings that Luke goes on to describe. And in the midst of it all, unprecedented numbers of people are believing and responding. Luke stresses the remarkable results: "more than ever"; "multitudes of both men and women." The gospel is bearing dramatic fruit. People are pouring into the kingdom.

But the language Luke uses is striking. He could have said that "more than ever believers were added *to the church*," or "multitudes of both men and women *became Christians*." But instead he says, "Believers were added *to the Lord*"—not added to the Lord's *followers* but added to the Lord *himself.* Once again, this is not how we would instinctively describe things. We talk about the church growing, but Luke talks about people being added to Jesus. *He*—not just a group of people or some kind of religious institution—is what they are joining. They are coming into *him.* When someone becomes a believer, that individual is being added to the Lord. If we find that a strange way to talk, it means we're not seeing something that is apparently obvious to Luke. If being a Christian is first and foremost to be "in Christ," then becoming a Christian is to be "added to the Lord."

Paul uses very similar language in how he describes people coming to faith. We tend to overlook the last chapter of Romans, as it is dominated by Paul sending greetings and messages to a long list of people. It is easy to skip over it. We don't know these people, and it feels a little bit like the end credits to the book. But these are names Paul wants us to know. They mean something to him and to the cause of the gospel he has just spent the fifteen previous chapters unpacking for us. This is not a distraction from the gospel; it is part of how it is so thoroughly grounded in Paul's life.

Among the twenty-seven names he mentions, Paul includes his friends Andronicus and Junia—"my kinsmen and my fellow prisoners. They are well known to the apostles, and they were in Christ before me" (Rom. 16:7). Andronicus and Junia were people Paul could strongly identify with. They are his kinsmen and fellow prisoners. But he also says they were "in Christ before me." They had been believers longer than Paul had. Like Luke in Acts 5, Paul defaults to expressing this reality in terms of their being joined to Christ. Being a Christian before Paul means they were "in Christ" before Paul.

The whole of Romans 16 is shot through with this perspective. Paul highlights Phoebe, "a servant of the church at Cenchreae," who will require the assistance of the believers Paul is writing to. So he calls on them not just to "welcome her" but to "welcome her in the Lord" (Rom. 16:1–2). She, like them, is also in this sphere of being in Christ, and it is to shape and define the way they receive her. Similarly, Prisca and Aquila, who have also labored alongside Paul, are described as "my fellow workers in Christ Jesus" (Rom. 16:3). The union in Christ they share with Paul also encapsulates the work they do for the Lord. In the same way, Ampliatus is Paul's "beloved in the Lord" (Rom. 16:8). Even Paul's affections are wrapped up in all this.

Given this pattern, we should not be surprised to see the way the language of being in Christ touches even seemingly mundane parts of Paul's writing, such as how he greets his readers. Paul opens his letter to the Philippians in this way: "To all the saints in Christ Jesus who are at Philippi, with the overseers and deacons" (Phil. 1:1). These Christians have a dual address. Geographically, they are in Philippi. But spiritually, they are in Christ. That Paul puts this spiritual location first suggests that it takes priority. If they had had GPS technology, it would have located them in what we know today as northeast Greece. But what really mattered was where they were located in relation to Jesus. These saints are "in" Christ. In fact (as we'll see), they can only be saints in the first place—people now set apart for Jesus—*because* they are in Christ. It's impossible to be a saint anywhere else. If they're in Christ, it's impossible *not* to be a saint. Being in Christ is not incidental; it defines who they are as believers. It is what is most fundamental to what it means to be a Christian.

These are just a handful of examples of where we find the language of being "in Christ" rather than the kind of language we typically use in Christian circles today. We could consider many dozens more. Being in Christ is central to how the New Testament describes the Christian life.

What "in Christ" Means

The centrality of this concept is explained by how foundational it is. The New Testament authors did not latch on to this language and push it to the forefront of their writing just out of personal preference. This isn't a case of "You like *tomayto*, and I like *tomahto*."[1] We need to have this idea at the heart of our thinking.

Pastor Rory Shiner gets at why this matters so much by imagining that we're at an airport wanting to fly to his home city of Perth, Australia:

What relationship do you need to have with that plane?

Would it help, for example, to be *under* the plane? To submit yourself to the plane's eminent authority in the whole flying-to-Perth caper?

Would it help to be *inspired* by the plane? You go to the airport, you watch it take off, and you whisper to yourself, "One day, I could do that too . . ."?

1   George Gershwin and Ira Gershwin, "Let's Call the Whole Thing Off," recorded March 3, 1937, Los Angeles, CA, Brunswick.

What about *following* the plane? You know the plane is going to Perth, and so it stands to reason that if you take note of the direction it goes, and pursue it as fast as your little legs will carry you, you too will end up in Perth.

Of course, the key relationship you need with the plane is not to be under it, behind it or inspired by it. You need to be *in* it.

Why? Because by being in the plane, what happens to the plane will also happen to you.

The question "Did you get to Perth?" will become part of a larger question, "Did the plane get to Perth?" If the answer to the second question is yes, and if you were in the plane, then what happened to the plane will also have happened to you.[2]

The same is true of us and Christ: if we are in Christ, what happens to him happens to us. Nevertheless, it is still a strange concept to us. What can it actually mean to say that someone is "in Christ"? Does Jesus have a zip code? Can I find him on Google Maps?

One thinks of Nicodemus's response to Jesus in this exchange:

Jesus answered him, "Truly, truly, I say to you, unless one is born again he cannot see the kingdom of God." Nicodemus said to him, "How can a man be born when he is old? Can he enter a second time into his mother's womb and be born?" (John 3:3–4)

Jesus just dropped the bombshell that to even see the kingdom of God, one would need a second birth, to be "born again"—literally, "born from above." This is not simply another attempt at the birth

2 Rory Shiner, *One Forever: The Transforming Power of Being in Christ* (Kingsford, AU: Matthias Media, 2012), 34.

all of us experienced when we entered this world; Jesus is saying there needs to be a new type of birth, one from heaven and not from earth.

But apparently missing that nuance, Nicodemus responds by pointing out the absurdity of trying to go through a second physical birth. The idea of any mature adult, let alone an older man, having to climb back into a mother's womb is certainly absurd in the extreme. It's the kind of thing online memes are made of.

But Jesus was talking not about another "normal" birth but about something quite different: a spiritual birth. Just as we need a physical birth to be able to experience life on this earth, so too we need a spiritual birth to be able to experience true life in God's kingdom.

We have a similar issue with understanding what it means to be "in Christ." For most of us, our only category for thinking about where we are is spatial. At this very moment, as I'm writing, I'm in a particular physical location—in a friend's house in the leafy village of Shincliffe, on the outskirts of the ancient city of Durham in northeast England. (A lovely place, by the way.) I'm not anywhere else. I'm "in Durham." To be "in Christ" does not contradict that. Jesus doesn't have a particular zip code that I need to find my way to. Just as it is possible to have both a physical birth and a spiritual birth, so too it is possible to have a physical, geographical location as well as a spiritual one. And just as I don't have to have been born of a particular woman to be able to go through a spiritual rebirth, so also I don't need to be in any particular place on earth to be able to find myself in Christ.

"In Christ" Illustrations

Perhaps because it is a somewhat alien concept to us, Scripture often unpacks our union with Christ using illustrations of more familiar things. Sometimes being told what something is *like* is a good way to begin understanding what that something is.

A Tree and Its Branches

Jesus speaks of his people's union with him as being like the relationship a branch has with a tree: "I am the vine; you are the branches" (John 15:5). We don't need to be familiar with vineyards specifically to get the point (though there are important reasons Jesus uses vineyards as an example here, as we'll see in due course). We know about the relationship a branch needs to have with a tree.

I've mentioned that as I'm writing this chapter, I'm staying at my friends' house just outside the city of Durham. Next to the house is the River Weir, which winds its way through County Durham. This particular stretch of the river is lined by tall oak and sycamore trees. On a previous visit a few months ago, I sat working and heard an unusually loud sound of creaking. I looked around to see if a piece of furniture was about to collapse, and just as I realized that the noise didn't seem to be coming from within the room, I heard a sudden crashing sound from outside. A huge branch had just torn itself off one of the larger oak trees. The branch itself was thicker than many of the sycamore trees around it and took out one of these on its way down. It's still there, some months later. Other than its size and conspicuous position, what makes this branch immediately identifiable is its lack of color. The woodland around it is alive in all shades of green, but the branch is a dull brown and its foliage withered and gray.

We know why. When a branch is removed from its tree, it dies. It loses connection with its source of life.

The same is true of our relationship with Jesus. We can't expect to flourish spiritually if we're apart from him. As Michael Reeves puts it, "The Vine holds nothing back from its branches, pouring all its life into them."[3] So if we disconnect from the vine, we—like that giant branch—will quickly wither and die. There is no spiritual life apart from Jesus.

Little wonder, then, that he goes on to talk about the need for us to "remain" or "abide" in him. Our being in Christ needs to be ongoing. Christianity, it turns out, is not about a quick one-off transaction with Jesus. The heart of the Christian life is Jesus himself. The only true life we can experience is drawn from him. We depend on him and have no spiritual life without him.

A Body and Its Head

Trees aren't the only things that have limbs. Bodies do too, and I'm depending on the relationship between a limb and my head to be able to write this. Paul notes,

> Rather, speaking the truth in love, we are to grow up in every way into him who is the head, into Christ, from whom the whole body, joined and held together by every joint with which it is equipped, when each part is working properly, makes the body grow so that it builds itself up in love. (Eph. 4:15–16)

We may be familiar with other scriptures in which the people of God are likened to a body, with each playing a different part. In those passages, the point is normally about our relationship

---

3   Michael Reeves, *Christ Our Life* (Milton Keynes, UK: Paternoster, 2014), 84.

with one another, how each of us is needed and each of us needs everyone else. But here the illustration is adjusted—we're not just like parts of a body relating to one another but like a body itself relating to its head. The focus is not our individual relationships to the rest of the church but our relationship as a church to Christ. We are the body, and he is the head. And while every part of the body has its own contribution to make, the head is utterly indispensable. We have prosthetic limbs for those who lose an arm or a leg, but there is no such thing as a prosthetic head.

So our relationship to Jesus is not just static (as that of a branch to a tree might seem to be): we are to "grow up in every way into him who is the head." The head is not just the source of our life; it shapes who we are and what we become. We are not just empowered by it but directed by it. The growth of the church— what "makes the body grow," in Paul's language—is ultimately its head. The whole body is involved—"each part is working properly"—but it is Christ alone who is behind the maturing and growth of the church.

A Spouse in a Marriage

The Bible repeatedly uses the language of a marriage to describe the relationship of God's people to the Lord, and in the New Testament this is applied to the church's relationship to Jesus. Collectively, the church is Christ's bride:

> "Therefore a man shall leave his father and mother and hold fast to his wife, and the two shall become one flesh." This mystery is profound, and I am saying that it refers to Christ and the church. (Eph. 5:31–32)

Then I saw a new heaven and a new earth, for the first heaven and the first earth had passed away, and the sea was no more. And I saw the holy city, new Jerusalem, coming down out of heaven from God, prepared as a bride adorned for her husband. (Rev. 21:1–2)

While the church is the bride of Christ, Paul also uses marital-related language to say something of the individual believer's relationship to Christ:

Or do you not know that he who is joined to a prostitute becomes one body with her? For, as it is written, "The two will become one flesh." But he who is joined to the Lord becomes one spirit with him. (1 Cor. 6:16–17)

In marriage, the man and woman become "one flesh." The two become one physically. Similarly, Paul shows us that the believer and Christ become one spiritually. We are "joined to the Lord"— that is what it means to become a Christian—and so become "one spirit with him." The oneness we have with Jesus is in some ways akin to the oneness a husband and wife experience (and which is so distorted by someone sleeping with a prostitute, as some in Corinth evidently needed to hear). The husband and wife in a marriage are made one without being fused together—they are still two individual people. So too with our relationship to Jesus. We are not absorbed or dissolved into Jesus. We do not lose our unique personality and distinctiveness. In fact, we become our truest selves by being in Christ.

Paul shows us that marriage points to Jesus and his people: "This mystery is profound, and I am saying that it refers to Christ and the church" (Eph. 5:32). We need to be clear which way around this analogy is meant to be understood. In our familiarity with the human institution of marriage, we tend to put it in the conceptual foreground and then think Paul is saying that our relationship to Jesus is a bit like *that*. But it is the other way around. The true reality is the gospel—our union with Christ and all that comes with it. The church's marital union with Jesus is the true and ultimate marriage, and our earthly marriages are something like *that*. So Paul is not merely saying that the pattern for marriage is a bit like what we have going on with Jesus; he's saying that if we don't think about our union with Christ in the right way, there is a danger we won't think about marriage in the right way. Our fullest understanding of marriage needs to be grounded in the doctrine of our union with Jesus. The "one flesh" relationship will be best understood as we honor and appreciate the dynamics of our "one spirit" relationship with the Lord.

Each of these illustrations—branches, bodies, brides—highlights a different aspect of this relationship to Jesus. He is our source of life, our directing and defining head, and one who is closer to us than any other relationship we can enjoy. John Stott sums it up neatly:

> The relationship which is thus depicted is something much more than a formal attachment or nodding acquaintance, something more even than a personal friendship; it is nothing less than a vital, organic, intimate union with Jesus Christ, involving a shared life and love.[4]

4 John Stott, *Life in Christ: A Guide for Daily Living* (1979; repr., London: Monarch Books, 2003), 41.

Christ is more needed, more close, and more vital than we ever realized.

Without an understanding of what it means to be in Christ, our view of the Christian life becomes blurry. The ideas will still be there, of course—we'll know that we're justified through the death of Christ alone, that we will one day join him in resurrection life, that in the meantime we're to commit ourselves to walking in holiness, and that all this is to be understood and worked through in the context of a local church. The pieces will be in place, but they won't fully cohere—they'll seem like separate elements, each of which we admire in its own way but which, like Lego bricks poured out onto the table, are meant to fit together and make a whole. Union with Christ is the lens through which all these parts of the Christian life can be seen most sharply and beautifully.

2

Blessed in Christ

*Blessed be the God and Father of our Lord Jesus
Christ, who has blessed us in Christ with every
spiritual blessing in the heavenly places.*

EPHESIANS 1:3

IT'S A FESTIVE TRADITION in my family to continue to receive a
Christmas stocking long after you've left home as an adult. I don't
always get to open it on Christmas Day itself (depending on where
I am), but at some point, when there's an appropriate opportunity
with my parents, we'll get to it. As it happens, even though it's a
few days before Christmas as I write this, I've just opened it.

Much of the content of those stockings has changed over the
decades. There are things I've grown out of—joke books, toy cars,
and Lego bricks. Other things are now somewhat obsolete for
me—postage stamps, cassette tapes, a new pencil case for high
school. The actual physical stocking itself has been replaced a few

times over the years. I don't know how many we've gone through by now. But there are some things that remain exactly the same from year to year: a particular assortment of Cadbury chocolates, a few pairs of Star Wars socks, some deodorant (I now realize I haven't changed my deodorant brand in thirty years), and, at the very bottom, a nectarine.

To be honest, this last item wasn't always the most exciting for me growing up—fruit doesn't really compete with chocolate, after all. Even today, I'm not a huge fan. But it's still a necessary part of the overall mix. It is tradition, and the stocking would be incomplete without it. Whether I get excited by it is beside the point.

We get to enjoy lots of amazing gifts in the Christian life. We have the precious assurance of sins forgiven. We receive the comforting presence of the Holy Spirit in our lives, making us more like Christ. We're given the gift of fellowship, finding ourselves part of a new and life-giving spiritual community. And we're granted eternal life, with the glorious prospect of the age to come. As we unpack all that comes to us through Christ, it can feel like pulling one amazing gift after another out of an incredible stocking.

And if that's the case, then our union with Christ might feel like the tangerine. It's not what we were necessarily looking for but something that evidently needed to be there, even if it doesn't seem as enticing as everything else. Maybe that's how you feel about the topic of this book—not something you might have thought you needed but something you're quite willing to deal with now that it's in front of you.

The fact is that our union with Christ is not one further item in our spiritual stocking—a discrete, separate gift we could almost miss, lying there at the very bottom. *It is more like the actual stocking itself.* It is through union with Christ that we receive all these other things. Without it, we receive none of them.

Abounding Blessings

Paul alerts us to the encompassing nature of union with Christ in how he opens his letter to the Ephesians:

> Paul, an apostle of Christ Jesus by the will of God,
>
> To the saints who are in Ephesus, and are faithful in Christ Jesus:
>
> Grace to you and peace from God our Father and the Lord Jesus Christ.
>
> Blessed be the God and Father of our Lord Jesus Christ, who has blessed us in Christ with every spiritual blessing in the heavenly places. (Eph. 1:1–3)

We can't help but notice that union with Christ is present even in the greeting. The Christians he is writing to are not just "the saints who are in Ephesus" (which puts them in modern-day Turkey for us); they're also those who "are faithful in Christ Jesus." Paul can barely make it one sentence without referencing our place in Christ.

But as he then begins the main body of the letter, he *really* puts it front and center. He launches into what is about to be a long, single sentence in the original Greek, covering Ephesians 1:3–14 in our translations. Paul is going to whisk us through our election by God even before the beginning of time, our adoption into God's family, our redemption and forgiveness of sins, our enjoyment of the Holy Spirit, and more. Part of the reason Paul keeps extending this one sentence seems to be that he's so caught up in what he's unpacking, as though he loses track of time. He is pulling out blessing after blessing, not so much for our analysis as for our wonder.

But framing it all is this key statement:

> Blessed be the God and Father of our Lord Jesus Christ, who has blessed us in Christ with every spiritual blessing in the heavenly places. (Eph. 1:3)

So many key truths come tumbling out of this one verse.

Blessing God

First, Paul says that *God is to be blessed*. This is not just the start of Paul's sentence; it is the start of all theology. Everything we're going to think about has its beginning here. All that is ours in Christ flows from this idea: the God of the Bible is a God who is to be blessed.

This might seem unusual. We tend to think of blessing as coming *from* God rather than being directed *to* him. And in a moment Paul will indeed talk about just how God *has* blessed us. But prior to the blessing he bestows is the blessing he deserves. Whatever else might need to be said about God, we need to know that he is supremely *blessable*.

What does it mean to bless God? We obviously can't give God anything he doesn't already have. Blessing him isn't adding to him in any way or filling up his self-esteem. God in himself lacks nothing—he is sufficient and complete.

To bless God is to *praise* him. The kind of blessing Paul calls for here is frequently heard throughout the Bible. Here are just three quick examples:

Blessed be the LORD, the God of Shem;
    and let Canaan be his servant. (Gen. 9:26)

Jethro said, "Blessed be the LORD, who has delivered you out of the hand of the Egyptians and out of the hand of Pharaoh and has delivered the people from under the hand of the Egyptians." (Ex. 18:10)

The LORD lives, and blessed be my rock,
    and exalted be the God of my salvation. (Ps. 18:46)

It's not about what God lacks but about what he *deserves*. In Psalm 18, "blessed" is paired with "exalted"—both go together. To bless God is to praise him.

The same psalm opens with the words "I love you, O LORD, my strength" (Ps. 18:1). Many of us default into seeing God in terms of what we're supposed to give him, as though scriptural calls to worship are simply about giving respect to the "office" of deity. But when the Bible speaks of God's worthiness, it often does so in terms of his goodness. He is not an abstract authority we have to give deference to; he is one whose being and ways should evoke wonder, awe, love, and delight.

I missed this for many years of my life. As I was growing up, my knowledge of God was limited to the handful of scriptures and hymns we were exposed to in religious studies classes and school assemblies. But it was all rather austere and dutiful. God seemed just a matter of obligation.

So we must be careful not to mishear what is being said in Ephesians. By calling us to bless God, Paul is not asking us to get our religious chores done before we can go out to play. He's inviting us into something wonderfully joyous.

We praise what we most delight in. I share a house with a dear friend who, within minutes of meeting someone, will bring up his favorite TV detective show to see if that person has seen it. We're all a bit like this with our favorite things—books, movies, songs, restaurants. My housemate is under no contractual obligation with the production company to tell everyone to watch *Broadchurch*. He just can't help himself. He wants others to share what he has enjoyed.

We do it with people too. When someone stuns us with a wonderful expression of kindness or a genuinely worthy achievement, we *have* to tell others about it. Such praise is not a requirement; it's a compulsion within us. We can't *not* praise the praiseworthy. C. S. Lewis nails it: "I think we delight to praise what we enjoy because the praise not merely expresses but completes the enjoyment; it is its appointed consummation."[1]

This is what Paul is talking about. Our blessing of God is grounded in God's blessing of us. But we must not think that this is some sort of transactional arrangement, as though we bless God *so that* he blesses us, our praise of him simply feeding coins into the meter so that we can remain parked in his favor. No, we praise God for the very way he is. Praising him is something we *get* to do; it is the reward, not the fee.

1   C. S. Lewis, *Reflections on the Psalms* (1958; repr., London: Fount, 1977), 81.

This is not the God people tend to imagine. Theologian N. T. Wright recalls making this very distinction to skeptical university students:

> For seven years I was College Chaplain at Worcester College, Oxford. Each year I used to see the first year undergraduates individually for a few minutes, to welcome them to the college and make a first acquaintance. Most were happy to meet me; but many commented, often with slight embarrassment, "You won't be seeing much of me; you see, I don't believe in god."
>
> I developed a stock response: "Oh, that's interesting. Which god is it you don't believe in?" This used to surprise them; they mostly regarded the word *God* as univocal, always meaning the same thing. So they would stumble out a few phrases about the god they didn't believe in: a being who lived up in the sky, looking down disapprovingly at the world, occasionally intervening to do miracles, sending bad people to hell while allowing good people to share his heaven. Again, I had a stock response for this very common "spy-in-the-sky" theology: "Well, I'm not surprised you don't believe in that god. I don't believe in that god either."[2]

The real God, when we look at him on his terms, is surprising to us. He's a God we *treasure*. To say "Blessed be God" is a way of saying that the truest response to God is *celebration*. When to our hearts he is no longer worthy to be blessed, it is a sure sign that we are not thinking about the God of Ephesians 1:3.

2   Marcus J. Borg and N. T. Wright, *The Meaning of Jesus: Two Visions* (New York: Harper-Collins, 1999), 157.

Spiritual Blessings

Paul now shows us a particular reason why this God is to be blessed—he has blessed us:

> Blessed be the God and Father of our Lord Jesus Christ, who has blessed us in Christ with every spiritual blessing in the heavenly places. (Eph. 1:3)

Let's think about these words.

"Blessed by God" has become a somewhat saccharine phrase in many places today. It can be shorthand for feeling materially privileged or above-average happy. It's the kind of thing people attribute getting an Oscar to. Those sorts of things are not bad in and of themselves, and all material gifts we enjoy should be acknowledged as coming ultimately from God. But Paul has a more specific focus—receiving "every spiritual blessing in the heavenly places."

These blessings are "spiritual"—they pertain to the person and work of the Holy Spirit. They are "in the heavenly places"—they have their origin in heaven and not on earth. And they are "in Christ"—not available anywhere other than by being found in him. So Paul is not simply talking about the good things of life in this world that anyone is able to enjoy; these spiritual blessings are unique to Christians.

Paul goes on to list them:

> Blessed be the God and Father of our Lord Jesus Christ, who has blessed us in Christ with every spiritual blessing in the heavenly places, even as he chose us in him before the foundation of the

world, that we should be holy and blameless before him. In love he predestined us for adoption to himself as sons through Jesus Christ, according to the purpose of his will, to the praise of his glorious grace, with which he has blessed us in the Beloved. In him we have redemption through his blood, the forgiveness of our trespasses, according to the riches of his grace, which he lavished upon us, in all wisdom and insight making known to us the mystery of his will, according to his purpose, which he set forth in Christ as a plan for the fullness of time, to unite all things in him, things in heaven and things on earth.

In him we have obtained an inheritance, having been predestined according to the purpose of him who works all things according to the counsel of his will, so that we who were the first to hope in Christ might be to the praise of his glory. In him you also, when you heard the word of truth, the gospel of your salvation, and believed in him, were sealed with the promised Holy Spirit, who is the guarantee of our inheritance until we acquire possession of it, to the praise of his glory. (Eph. 1:3–14)

If we were to, so to speak, click on "spiritual blessing," this passage is what would come up. And it is magnificent. We can't go through all of it. This one sentence in the original Greek would take a whole book to properly unpack—and a whole lifetime to fully appreciate. But we can pull out some of the things Paul is looking at here.

Election

Paul talks about being *chosen*. This language understandably raises lots of questions among thoughtful believers—*Why me? Why not others who don't seem to know Christ? Does this mean I have no agency in any of this?* Paul doesn't stop to consider all that here (he looks at some of these concerns in Rom. 9–11). He is giving us a whistle-stop tour, an overview. And the purpose is not to answer all our questions but to fire our appreciation.

We've been chosen. God actually means to have us around. We didn't stumble into this by some accident on our part or because of some clerical error in the heavenlies. The presence of God in our lives was always his idea. He meant to be involved with you.

This is reassuring and humbling. God chose us "before the foundation of the world" (Eph. 1:4). It wasn't as if God was tracking our progress and weighing up whether we would be good enough for him. The choice was his before we had done anything, before even the universe was around. So we can't claim any credit.

Moreover, we're chosen to be "holy and blameless before him" (Eph. 1:4). Think about that.

Imagine that one day you're walking through a busy shopping mall. A cluster of people with clipboards are grabbing selected passersby for an exclusive offer. They let others pass, but one of them sees you and pulls you aside. You have been *chosen*. Sounds great, right? But it turns out that they are advertising a makeover service and are offering you a special deal on one. Now it feels much less flattering. Someone choosing you for a makeover says something about your present state of appearance. And so it is with God's choosing of us. He has chosen us to be holy and blameless precisely because we are naturally *unholy* and *blameworthy*.

But here's Paul's point: God having chosen us before we were even aware of who he was is a huge blessing. Our life with him has always been entirely in God's hands, not ours. It was never down to me but to him. We're thousands of years too late to blow it. I can rest in his sovereign choosing of me.

Adoption

Paul also talks about *adoption*. We have not just been theoretically saved but actually grafted into God's family.

This is a deeper category of salvation than many of us tend to think about. It is easy to conceive of God forgiving us in the sense of no longer having anything against us. But the category of adoption reminds us that the message of the gospel is not merely "Off you go" but "In you come." A lifeguard plucking a drowning individual out of the water takes her back to dry land; he doesn't then start a new life with her. But this is what God does. He doesn't keep his saved people at arm's length; he opens up his inner life to us. We are adopted. God is now our Father. We marvel not just at what we've been saved from but at what we've been saved into.

Knowledge

There's more. Another blessing we tend not to consider is the blessing of *knowledge*. Look at what Paul goes on to say:

> . . . making known to us the mystery of his will, according to his purpose, which he set forth in Christ as a plan for the fullness of time, to unite all things in him, things in heaven and things on earth. (Eph. 1:9–10)

God gives us the knowledge of his will; he makes it known to us.

This is a blessing because we hate being kept out of the loop. We hate it when we know something is going on but are not allowed to know what that something is. When we were kids, things were kept from us because we weren't old enough to be given the full story. Sometimes as adults, things are kept from us in the workplace, say, because we're not senior enough. But when someone lets you in on what's *really* going on, it's profoundly meaningful: a friend opens up about something he's dealing with and hasn't really shared with others; your boss takes you to one side to tell you what's happening behind the scenes, what plans are in the pipeline for the company, why this or that particular person has been hired or let go. It means something.

What God is letting us in on is not trivial. We've seen interviews with actors about some upcoming blockbuster in which it's obvious they are not allowed to actually tell you anything about what will happen in the movie. They're in the catch-22 of having to do publicity, to be talking nonstop about the movie, while not being able to divulge anything of significance about it. So you just get generic platitudes. But that's not the case with God. What he tells us about is deeply significant. It concerns his plan for "all things . . . in heaven and on earth."

Paul describes it as a "mystery." In the Bible, the word "mystery" is not something you can't explain or that doesn't make sense; it is something that was hidden but has now been revealed. It's a bit like a Christmas present: it has sat there under the tree for days in the run-up to Christmas. You can read the label, so you know it's for you. You can see the shape, even pick it up to find out what it feels like and how heavy it is. But it's only when you get to unwrap it that the mystery is finally revealed.

This is how it is with God's plan. It has always been there but has been somewhat hidden. There were hints and promises along the way, but it's only now, with the coming of Christ, that we can pull the wrapping off and really see what God is up to in the universe. Only in Christ do we have a fuller picture; only in Christ can we begin to make sense of how all things will be finally united in Jesus himself.

What we're being let in on here is a blessing to be let in on. In her memoir *Becoming*, Michelle Obama describes the moment when the newly elected Barack Obama was taken aside by some officials and told the nation's secrets. She reflected on the heaviness of this moment. Whatever he had been told was privileged information, to be sure, but it was also burdening information. The weight of the office was now fully on him.[3]

But what God reveals to us doesn't weigh us down; it lifts us up. Paul can describe Christians as those who "hope in Christ" (Eph. 1:12). God's plan gives us *hope* in a world of uncertainty. We know where things are headed. We know that there is a plan behind all that is unfolding around us. We know that one day all things will finally be united in Jesus, in full harmony and peace.

Blessing through Union

We could go on. Paul talks about redemption and forgiveness (Eph. 1:7), our inheritance (1:11), our reception of the Holy Spirit (1:13), and the guarantee he is of what is to come (1:14). But the main point is that *all this comes through Christ*. We've received these blessings "in Christ" (1:3). All these gifts come to us in the stocking of our union with Jesus.

Two things immediately flow from this conglomeration of blessings. First, in Jesus we lack nothing at all. Paul makes this so

---

3 Michelle Obama, *Becoming* (New York: Crown, 2018), 286.

very clear: "*every* spiritual blessing in the heavenly places" (Eph. 1:3). There is no spiritual blessing we miss out on in Christ. In him we have everything we need. We don't need to go looking for supplemental blessings anywhere outside him. What he has for us is wonderfully comprehensive. We have the whole package. Every spiritual blessing.

Second, outside Christ we can enjoy none of these spiritual blessings. We can enjoy the gifts of what theologians call common grace—God's goodness to all people irrespective of their relationship to Jesus. We can enjoy happy homes, meaningful work, wonderful friendships, the beauty of this world, and so on. But there are no spiritual blessings to be enjoyed outside Christ. John Calvin puts it this way, "As long as Christ remains outside of us, and we are separated from him, all that he has suffered and done for the salvation of the human race remains useless and of no value for us."[4]

This is a very binary way of thinking, and we tend not to think in such ways today. We want to blur the boundaries and merge the categories. We know people who are not Christians but who seem spiritually sincere. They spend time in meditation or mindfulness or reflection. They know the universe is bigger than they are. They may even claim to believe in some form of higher power. They are committed to doing good for others. They know that there is a spiritual dimension to reality and that ignoring it is injurious to us. Surely that all counts for something? They might not have everything we enjoy as Christians, but can we really say they have no spiritual blessings?

We must. We can recognize the general benefits that flow from being spiritually aware, from seeking a healthy balance and

---

4   John Calvin, *Institutes of Christian Religion*, ed. John T. McNeill, trans. Ford Lewis Battles, 2 vols., Library of Christian Classics 20–21 (Louisville: Westminster, 1960), 1:537.

perspective to life. But these are not the spiritual blessings Paul is talking about here in Ephesians. If it can't be found in Christ, it is not truly "spiritual" at all.

The Case of Cornelius

Cornelius, whom we meet in the book of Acts, is a helpful case in point:

> At Caesarea there was a man named Cornelius, a centurion of what was known as the Italian Cohort, a devout man who feared God with all his household, gave alms generously to the people, and prayed continually to God. About the ninth hour of the day he saw clearly in a vision an angel of God come in and say to him, "Cornelius." And he stared at him in terror and said, "What is it, Lord?" And he said to him, "Your prayers and your alms have ascended as a memorial before God. And now send men to Joppa and bring one Simon who is called Peter." (Acts 10:1–5)

There are so many positives we're given about Cornelius here: he's devout, he's a God-fearer, he is generous in what he gives to others, and he's faithful in prayer. He appears to be in a spiritually healthier place than many fellow Christians we might be able to think of. We're even told that his prayers and giving have come before God as a memorial. A few verses later, we're told that he's "an upright and God-fearing man, who is well spoken of by the whole Jewish nation" (Acts 10:22). Sure, he's technically a pagan, but he sounds as though he's spiritually "in," right?

As it happens, no.

Cornelius obeys the angel in the vision and sends for Peter, who shares the message of Jesus with him. Peter later goes on to recount these events, how Cornelius

> had seen the angel stand in his house and say, "Send to Joppa and bring Simon who is called Peter; he will declare to you a message by which you will be saved, you and all your household." As I [i.e., Peter] began to speak, the Holy Spirit fell on them just as on us at the beginning. (Acts 11:13–15)

So this man, Cornelius—devout, God-fearing, generous, prayerful, upright, well-spoken of—still needed to be *saved*. His religious earnestness, his spiritual discipline, his obvious goodness as a man—none of it was enough. He was outside Christ. Only by hearing the gospel and responding in faith could he truly come to find spiritual life in Jesus. It is sobering to think that even he needed to be in Christ. It is thrilling to consider how anyone can be joined to Christ through something as straightforward as proclaiming the message of Jesus.

Outside Jesus, we ultimately *have* nothing spiritually. Inside Jesus, we ultimately *lack* nothing spiritually. We have it all in Christ. Blessed we are. And blessed be God.

3

Saved in Christ

For as in Adam all die, so also in
Christ shall all be made alive.

I CORINTHIANS 15:22

ONE OF MY FAMILY'S more unusual Christmas traditions is to eat haggis for breakfast the day after Christmas. As if the culinary onslaught of Christmas Day itself wasn't enough, here we are, barely minutes into the morning, ingesting offal, suet, and oats (with a fried egg on top).

It may not be a common tradition, but it is a telling one. It is one of the few tangible reminders that my family has Scottish roots. At some point in the early twentieth century, the family made its way down from north of the border, and ever since, we've found ourselves being born in southeast England. It wasn't a decision I was involved in, obviously, and given the choice, I might have preferred growing up around the rugged hills of Galloway and speaking with a lilting Scottish accent.

The fact is that much in our lives is shaped by decisions made by our forebears. The choices of previous family members have determined many details of our lives even before we've begun deciding anything ourselves. It is not always comfortable to think about (we like to think of ourselves as masters of our own individual lives), but it is incontrovertibly true. We find ourselves to be the product of other people's choices. My family proffering grilled haggis every December 26 is evidence of that.

What is true of our physical family is also true of our spiritual family. One of my Scottish forebears made a decision, and ever since, successive generations have been born rooting for the wrong side when watching *Braveheart*. And one of my spiritual forebears made a decision that has meant that all of us ever since have found ourselves born very far from home. You won't make much sense of my family Christmas unless you understand where we've come from, and none of us will make much sense of our own lives unless we understand what happened way back at the very beginning of our spiritual family tree.

Before we were in Christ as Christians, we were not just drifting about unattached. We were *in Adam*—defined and shaped by what he did. And that is why we needed saving. Understanding Adam is key if we are to appreciate and understand what Christ has done for us.

Adam's Act

Paul summarizes the defining moment this way:

> Therefore, just as sin came into the world through one man, and death through sin, and so death spread to all men because all sinned . . . (Rom. 5:12)

The first part describes what happened *historically*: through one man sin entered what had been a pristine world. The second part helps us see what was happening *theologically*: all of us sinned.

Adam sinned. If we are at all familiar with the story of Genesis 1–3, we will know this. Adam was given enormous privileges and freedoms in the garden of Eden. It was already established that Eden was a place of abundant and attractive provision, and Adam was free to avail himself of it all—with one exception. The fruit from one particular tree was forbidden. This was no arbitrary rule thrown down by God just for the sake of having some boundaries. This particular tree represented his right to be God. It was in the middle of the garden, to be acknowledged and understood by Adam as the basis on which he could enjoy all the blessings God had for him. And it also needed to be respected by Adam, reminding him that he lived in *God's* good world.

But Adam disobeyed. With his wife, Eve, he ate from the tree, breaking God's command. He rebelled. Or, to use Paul's terminology, he *sinned*. And this is the significant bit: by doing so, Adam was actually introducing sin into the world.

It is beyond our imagining, but this world was once without sin. Through Adam's act of disobedience, sin came into the world. In other words, that one act of defiance had enormous and far-reaching consequences. It was not a self-contained, one-off act.

I remember reading about some of the early European settlers in Australia and their hapless attempts to introduce new species to the land. The most famous of these was the introduction of rabbits. Some chap liked being in Australia and also liked rabbits, and he had the bright idea of bringing the two together. I'm sure it would have seemed completely innocuous at the time. A few cute bunnies hopping about with an Australian backdrop would be lovely. What's the harm? But the result was ecological cataclysm. He unwittingly introduced something that the ecosystem was not prepared for and that quickly overwhelmed it.

Adam also introduced something into Eden that quickly overwhelmed the whole spiritual ecosystem—as God had warned it would. Sin came into the world and, like virulent rabbits, quickly multiplied out of control and made its presence felt in every far-flung corner. Adam's act was catastrophic.

Enter Death

But it did not end there. Sin was not the only thing to come. Hot on its heels, death followed.

God had always said disobedience would bring with it death, and now it certainly did. You can't have one without the other.

A while ago a good friend asked if I would look after his dog for a couple of weeks while he was away on a trip. I was eager to: Riley is a golden retriever who's been impeccably trained. I was looking forward to having him in the house.

The day came, and my friend talked me through all the logistics of keeping a dog: when his mealtimes would be, what to feed him, when to walk him, what the ground rules were, what were his favorite toys, and so on. I nodded along enthusiastically. But then he brought out some small plastic bags and explained how they were to be used. I hadn't thought about this part. But it turns out you can't have the dog without the poop. One is the inevitable outcome of the other. All the food Riley was to be fed was going to lead to *something*, and over the next week or so, many, many of those bags became full of that something.

You can't have the dog without the poop. And you can't have sin without death. It follows just as inevitably and just as unpleasantly. With one act, Adam had brought both sin and death into the world.

The Whole Cast

But Adam's sin was not just calamitous for him and his world; it has plunged all of us into sin and death. Paul makes a very clear connection between what Adam did and us:

> Therefore, just as sin came into the world through one man, and death through sin, and so death spread to all men *because all sinned* . . . (Rom. 5:12)

When Adam sinned, we all sinned. We need to understand what that means because it shapes precisely why we need to be saved and what form and scope that salvation needs to have.

Paul is not just saying that Adam kicked off a trend that all of us have since followed, like that ice-bucket challenge from a few years ago. No, it is not just that Adam has set a bad example and that we've all followed suit. It goes much deeper than that, and Paul shows us how just a few verses later. Still talking about Adam's first act of sin, he writes,

> For as by the one man's disobedience the many were made sinners . . . (Rom. 5:19)

The point is this: by Adam's act, all of us are *constituted* sinners. His sin *made* us sinners. He is not just our forebear but our representative—what he did is reckoned to us.

This sounds very wrong to our Western ears. We cherish our individualism and with it our individual responsibility. How can it possibly be fair for what Adam did to end up determining our own status and fate?

But the fact is that we do see this concept of representation in all sorts of ways today. As I write this, a significant rugby contest is underway. I don't follow rugby, so I've had to actually look up who is playing. It turns out my own country, England, is playing, and it looks as if it could go either way. But this is the significant point: the English rugby team isn't the English rugby team because it's *from* England but because it *represents* England. What they do regarding rugby is applied to all of us as a nation. If England wins and wipes the floor with all the opposition, people like me can say, "*We* won! *We* English are amazing at this game!" Someone like me, who knows virtually nothing about the game and almost didn't know it was happening, can take credit and pride in what someone else has done and I could never do—all because the England team plays on behalf of the rest of us. Whatever the result of the match, it will be applied to me. That's how these things work.

And it's how it worked in the garden of Eden. Adam was our spiritual representative. What he did with the commands of God, he did representing all humanity. It makes no difference whether we believe in this or agreed to it, just as it makes no difference if I have any interest in rugby. Adam acted on behalf of the whole human race. What he did was applied to us all. When he disobeyed, we were all at that point "made sinners" (Rom. 5:19).

It is very important to grasp this concept because it gets to the heart of our spiritual condition. Being made sinners does not just mean that, in some abstract way, we now have a mark against us, as if somewhere out there in the universe is a spiritual blacklist with our name on it. When Paul says that we were made sinners, he means in our *nature* and not just in our *status*. We *are* now sinners. In this respect it is a little different from the sports analogy above. England triumphing at rugby would give me bragging rights about it. But it wouldn't suddenly make me able to play rugby. It might encourage me to take up the sport (not likely), but it wouldn't improve my natural hand-eye coordination or in any way make me want to run around in the mud on a cold winter's morning.

But Adam's representation goes much deeper. It has shaped who we now find ourselves to be and how we behave. It might sound unfair or incredible to many today. We might instinctively respond in disbelief. But there are two things that prove it is, in fact, the case—that prove beyond doubt that Adam's act has been applied to us. We may not like it, but Paul can prove it:

> Therefore, just as sin came into the world through one man, and death through sin, and so death spread to all men *because all sinned* . . . (Rom. 5:12)

First, *we sin*. All of us. Without exception. The best way to disprove Paul's point would simply be to live without sinning. That would immediately settle it. But we don't because we can't. And those who think they can have so overridden their own natural conscience or loosened their grip on reality that we tend to give them a very wide berth. Because of Adam, it is our nature to sin, and therefore we do.

We need to get this the right way around: we are not constituted sinners because at various points along the way we've committed sins; we commit individual sins because *we are already* by nature sinners. Our acts of sin are not the reason we're sinners but merely the proof of it. You lie to someone because by nature, in your heart, you are a liar. Lying doesn't make you a liar; it proves you are a liar. Sinning doesn't make you a sinner; it proves you already are one. Every single day you and I prove Paul's point.

But there is a difference between Adam and the rest of us. He *became* a sinner. There was a point before he first sinned when he was not yet a sinner. But we have never been anything else. We were not born innocent and then at some stage became sinners. From our first moments of existence, we have had this sinful nature within us.

Again, this may sound unfair. But—also again—experience bears this out.

It is often observed that children do not need to be taught how to misbehave. No one has to tell them how to refuse to share or how to push others out of their way. It is instinctive and natural. Children are not innocent; all of us alike are born sinners. There is no moment of our natural existence when we are not in Adam.

The second proof that Paul's wider point is true is that *we all die*:

Therefore, just as sin came into the world through one man, and death through sin, and so *death spread to all men because all sinned* . . . (Rom. 5:12)

That we are sinners through Adam is seen in that we sin. It is also seen in that we die. Death comes to us all *because* all of us have sinned. Death is universal among us because sin is universal among us.

I take it from this that death was never intended to be part of our human experience. Paul is clear that death came through sin.

46

It was not part of God's original plan for us to die. Adam and Eve were meant to live in the presence of the tree of life forever. God's warning to Adam would make no sense otherwise. Adam had been told not to eat the fruit of the tree of the knowledge of good and evil and that if he did so, he would receive this sentence: "You shall surely die" (Gen. 2:17). Death was introduced as the punishment for sin precisely because it was not a normal part of human experience. It came through sin.

And therefore, all of us die. There is no escaping it. Just as none of us can live sinlessly (and disprove Paul's first assertion about sin coming to us all through Adam), so too none of us can live "deathlessly" (which would disprove Paul's second assertion that death comes to us all through sin). Just as my eating cooked sheep's offal every late December is tangible evidence of my family's Scottish background, so too our depravity and our mortality are evidence of our Adamic background. It might be a hard doctrine for some to accept, but it's one of the easiest to prove. There are around eight billion pieces of evidence for it walking around the planet today.

But if we deeply accept what the Bible is showing us, it can transform us. Paul is ultimately pointing us to something positive. We need to understand what it means to be in Adam if we are to grasp why we need to be in Christ. Adam's sin plunged humanity into spiritual crisis. But without knowing it, Adam was also establishing something of a pattern:

> Yet death reigned from Adam to Moses, even over those whose sinning was not like the transgression of Adam, *who was a type of the one who was to come.* (Rom. 5:14)

Paul is making a distinction between those sinning before Moses and those sinning afterward. Both are forms of sinning, but the difference is that through Moses God gave his people his law. Like Adam, their ensuing disobedience was against explicit verbal instructions. Those before Moses and after Adam were not breaking written commands but still nevertheless sinned, and so the outcome was the same: death reigned. But the point is what Paul goes on to say at the end of the verse: Adam, he tells us, is a type of the one to come, Jesus Christ. In other words, Adam provides something of a template of what Christ would come to do.

In my twenties, I shared an apartment with a couple of friends. Two of us developed the habit of randomly jumping out and scaring each other. One night, as I was just going to bed, I spotted him hiding in a window cavity in my bedroom. Thin curtains veiled him, and a bright street lamp shone just outside, so without knowing it, he was perfectly silhouetted. Needless to say, I tiptoed up to him and made the most of the opportunity.

Paul is saying that when we look at what Adam did and how it affected us, we discover an outline of the shape of what Jesus came to do. But in the case of Jesus, as we'll see, the effect was the opposite of Adam's. If the bad news is what has happened as a result of Adam being our representative, the good news is in knowing that there is another representative whose life was very different from Adam's.

Adam's Foil

Adam is a type of Christ. But having just made the comparison, Paul immediately points out the differences between them. It is as if he cannot bear to have the similarity between these two men lingering even for a moment without it being qualified. And so having shown us a way that they are alike, he now stresses the ways in which they are profoundly different:

> But the free gift is not like the trespass. For if many died through one man's trespass, much more have the grace of God and the free gift by the grace of that one man Jesus Christ abounded for many. (Rom. 5:15)

Yes, Adam and Jesus are alike: both—through one act—have shaped the destiny of many. But in every other respect, they are as different as can be. Paul lists out some of the many ways, concluding,

> For as by the one man's disobedience the many were made sinners, so by the one man's obedience the many will be made righteous. (Rom. 5:19)

Adam acted in *disobedience*, but Christ acted in full *obedience*. Both faced difficult choices in a garden: Adam in Eden, Jesus in Gethsemane. Both went to a tree: the forbidden tree for Adam, the wooden cross for Jesus. But whereas Adam brought sin and death into the world, Jesus has brought about forgiveness and new life.

Paul shows how different these outcomes are:

> And the free gift is not like the result of that one man's sin. For the judgment following one trespass brought condemnation, but the free gift following many trespasses brought justification. (Rom. 5:16)

49

In one case, the result was condemnation: humanity under the just judgment of God and sentenced to death. But now through Christ there is justification: people declared to be righteous in his sight.

Yet it is a difference not just of outcome but also of power. Condemnation through Adam followed *one* trespass, but the acquittal through Jesus followed *many* trespasses. Jesus's act for us is not merely the equal and opposite of Adam's; it is far greater than his. Paul continues:

> For if, because of one man's trespass, death reigned through that one man, much more will those who receive the abundance of grace and the free gift of righteousness reign in life through the one man Jesus Christ. (Rom. 5:17)

Through Adam, as we've seen, death reigned. Through Christ, what reigns? We would expect Paul to say that "life reigns," completing the symmetry. But he doesn't. It is not life that now reigns as the alternative to death, it is *those who receive grace* from Christ. *They* reign through him. What an extraordinary reversal. Jesus does not just act as our champion, defeating our enemies and then passing to us some of the spoils of his victory; he actually *shares* his victorious rule with us. We now reign in life through him!

What Jesus has done is the opposite of what Adam has done but is *far greater*. The two are not symmetrical.

Having established this point, Paul can now go on to finish unpacking how it is that Adam is the "type of the one who was to come" (Rom. 5:14). We are no longer in any danger of thinking the two are in any way the *same*. But there are some key parallels.

In both cases, one act affects many people:

Therefore, as one trespass led to condemnation for all men, so one act of righteousness leads to justification and life for all men. (Rom. 5:18)

With one action, "all" are affected. Paul is not meaning by this that all people irrespective of their relationship to Christ will receive justification and life. The "all men" condemned through Adam are all those who are in Adam, and the "all men" justified through Christ are all those who are in Christ. Christ is the federal head of all those who come to him in faith, trusting him alone for salvation. The saving consequences of his one act are applied to all who call on his name.

But as we saw with Adam's sin, it is not just our status that is changed by being represented by him; it is also our nature. We were made sinners; now through Christ we are made righteous:

For as by the one man's disobedience the many were made sinners, so by the one man's obedience the many will be made righteous. (Rom. 5:19)

We are declared righteous now in *status*, and his ongoing work in our lives is to make us *inwardly righteous* as we become more like him. Those *declared* righteous in Jesus are *made* righteous through his Spirit. What a wonderful prospect this is for us. As we come to Christ for the first time, we come aware of our need for him, of our natural unrighteousness. As we progress in the Christian life, getting to know the teachings of Jesus, we become even more aware of the depths of our sin within. And yet as we grow in awareness of how unlike Jesus we are, we receive the assurance of knowing that he is at work to make us more and more like him.

In Adam we were doomed, but in Christ we are saved!

Implications

These truths are enormously practical. They shape how we are to see ourselves and others.

Human Identity

We tend to view people through any number of lenses. We think of one another in terms of ethnicity, gender, culture, or economic bracket. We think of people as being young or old, rich or poor. We subdivide and categorize. We're not always aware we are doing it. The particular grid we place on people will vary according to who we are, and it changes over time.

As young children, we are often very interested in people's ages. We know our own exact age almost to the month, and we want to know how that compares to others. Upon seeing her great-grandmother, a five-year-old relative of mine exclaimed that this elderly lady must be at least *twenty-five* years old. During puberty, we may be especially mindful of other people's gender, as we become increasingly sexually aware. During the early days of our working life, we may be mindful of other people's economic status or livelihood, maybe even calculating where we all fit in the pecking order of our culture, or mindful of other people's marital status, wondering if they are in the same bracket as we are. There are any number of ways we can categorize and any number of priorities we might have in doing so.

But the most important distinction between people, the most fundamental truth about anyone, is *whether they are in Adam or in Christ.* This is what matters the most because this is what determines the most. We are all born by nature into Adam. And we can only be reborn into Christ. Our standing before God, our inner nature, and our eternal destiny all flow from which of these two men is our representative. Nothing in life determines more than this.

Marriage

It is this difference between being in Adam and being in Christ that explains why the Bible repeatedly teaches that Christians should not marry those outside the faith. Writing to widows considering further marriage, Paul says such people can marry whom they wish to, provided it is someone "in the Lord" (1 Cor. 7:39). This is the crucial identifying marker—not whether the other person has the right kind of look, the right kind of job, the right kind of tastes—but whether that person is in Christ. Elsewhere he writes that Christians should not be "unequally yoked" to unbelievers (2 Cor. 6:14). I think Paul had in mind a broader view than just sex and marriage, but the principle certainly applies to these areas. A Christian must not marry someone who is not a believer.

We mustn't misunderstand why this is so. Paul is not saying that Christians shouldn't marry unbelievers because he thinks all unbelievers must be bad and all Christians good. I know many very good non-Christians and a number of quite unpleasant Christians. No, the issue is not simply a matter of someone's observable behavior; it runs far deeper than that. A Christian and a non-Christian belong to entirely different realities. There is no spiritual overlap at all.

As Peter describes the people of God in his first letter, he calls them, among other things, "a chosen race" (1 Pet. 2:9). God's people are not just one more demographic, voting bloc, or option on a census form. We are a distinct *spiritual race*, one that transcends all the ethnic categories of this world. And Christians are not to marry outside this spiritual race (while being free to marry any ethnicity). If you are in Christ, you must marry only someone else who is in Christ. The animating core of who you are as a Christian is too distinct to be blended in such intimacy with someone who is not.

Compassion

Properly understood, these things should make us more compassionate. The very part of this we often find difficult—our helplessness through Adam—can soften our hearts to one another.

Adam's sin makes all who succeed him sinners by nature. The presence of sin in our lives is inevitable. We can't help it. It doesn't mean that we're not responsible or that there aren't consequences for our sin or that God isn't right to condemn and punish it. But it shows just how helpless we all are. We're sinners and can't be otherwise. When we see another person sin, we're watching him be the only thing he knows how to be. It doesn't make it less wrong, but it makes it all the more understandable. We can't snap ourselves out of this. We can only be reborn out of it.

This shapes how we see all humanity, even at its ugliest. It explains the world to us, showing us how even with unprecedented wealth, education, and technology, we can't seem to get our act together as a species. We may be cleverer, healthier, and cleaner, but we're not *better*. We see the ongoing pattern of sin, that inherent Adamness, repeating itself in each new generation. No human advances will get us out of this.

This doesn't mean that we don't do what we can to encourage social reform or to pursue justice and righteousness. God's common grace means we can do some things to restrain aspects of our sinfulness. We rejoice over efforts to abolish trafficking, racial discrimination, or abortion. But we do so knowing the deeper issue hasn't been resolved: sin is native to us, and sinners are going to sin.

Mission

Whenever I meet other people—no matter how different they are from me culturally or ethnically or economically—this lens of original sin helps me understand what they most need deep down. However bewildering another culture may be to me, the underlying substructure of the human heart is the same. Our birth certificates may state that we were born in London or Peshawar or Cape Town or São Paolo. But spiritually, we're all born in Adam.

However different people might be from us, however complex their background or issues in life, the fact is that we do know what they most fundamentally need—new birth through Christ. This is actually very liberating to know. In an increasingly multicultural world, we may find ourselves living in close proximity to communities vastly different from our own—communities that seem so hard for us to understand. We might be tempted to think that we could never really connect with them or relate to them. Their worldview is too different or their experiences too unlike anything we have ever gone through. We would never be able to truly bridge that gap.

Yet whatever complexities exist at the level of culture, at the level of their spiritual state we can understand others profoundly. They, like us, were born in Adam. We know what it is that they most fundamentally need. We can have confidence that the gospel can help and transform them.

Parenting

This teaching about being in Adam and being in Christ can be an encouragement for parents. Your child's sinfulness isn't just the result of your imperfections as a parent. Even if, somehow, you had made all the right parenting choices at every moment along the way, your child would still be a sinner.

A friend with a young child caught her trying to bite one of the friends she was playing with. He was distressed by this, of course, but also a little confused. Where had she picked up such a notion? He checked with his wife; she had no idea either. They had had to teach their daughter to use the potty, to walk, to brush her teeth, and a thousand other things. They hadn't had to teach her to sin. Biting someone out of frustration just came naturally, it seems. My friend described realizing this as a bit of a relief: not every crazy thing his children did was necessarily the result of bad parenting.

The best-raised child will still be fallen. No matter how "advanced" a human civilization becomes, its people will still share the same sinful state as those in the least civilized nation. It makes the gospel all the more urgent and all the more precious. Every human I set eyes on today (including the one in the mirror) has the same ultimate need and helplessness. By nature, we're all descendants of Adam, whatever is on the menu for our post-Christmas breakfast.

4

Justified in Christ

*For our sake he made him to be sin who knew no sin, so
that in him we might become the righteousness of God.*

2 CORINTHIANS 5:21

IT WAS THE MOST POWERFUL way I have ever seen God at
work. I was at an event for a group of Christian men in part of
the Caribbean. On the first day, I had been taken aback by the
hard-heartedness of many who were there. This particular group
embraced a culture of machismo, of invulnerability, of prowess.

But in just forty-eight hours, that all changed.

It was one older man who led the way. In the middle of one of
the sessions, he openly confessed sin in front of the whole gather-
ing, admitting ways he had been unloving to others. It was as if a
dam burst. A succession of many other delegates started following
suit, confessing similar and related shortcomings. In this kind
of culture, such raw and tearful honesty was uncommon, and

the whole room was deeply moved. Eventually, someone started singing, and the rest of the crowd quickly joined in. They were all singing in Spanish. A friend next to me offered to translate so that I could follow what they were singing. But I didn't need it. It was obvious what they were singing about, many in tears as they did so—the cross of Christ.

The cross has always been at the heart of our faith. Paul himself wrote, "For I decided to know nothing among you except Jesus Christ and him crucified" (1 Cor. 2:2). It lay at the heart of his confidence and formed the heart of his message. It has been so for believers ever since. Many of our church buildings are laid out in the shape of a cross. I'm not typically given to wearing jewelry, but I often wear a cross around my neck. We see crosses on church logos, on tombstones, sometimes on roadsides, on our Bibles, and we may have them decorating our walls. The cross is at once familiar and comforting.

The cross is where Christ paid for our sin and secured our atonement. We think of it as being the grounds of our forgiveness, the focus of our assurance, and the shape of our subsequent discipleship. It is all our hope in this world.

But should it be? Is it right to think of the cross in this way? Is the idea that Jesus died for our sin, taking the punishment we deserved, actually a *noble* idea?

An Immoral Cross?

Christopher Hitchens has long been my favorite atheist. He seemed willing to debate pretty much anyone, including many church leaders. He appeared to revel in the back-and-forth and, from what I could see, seemed fair and reasonable, readily conceding when he lost a debate.[1] He even appeared to get along with a number of the Christians he debated.[2]

But none of that took away from the strength of his arguments. Hitchens was fearless and formidable. One particular line of argument struck me forcefully the first time I came across it:

> I find something repulsive about the idea of vicarious redemption. I would not throw my numberless sins onto a scapegoat and expect them to pass from me; we rightly sneer at the barbaric societies that practice this unpleasantness in its literal form. There's no moral value in the vicarious gesture anyway. As Thomas Paine pointed out, you may if you wish take on another man's debt, or even to take his place in prison. That would be self-sacrificing. But you may not assume his actual crimes as if they were your own; for one thing you did not commit them and might have died rather than do so; for another this impossible action would rob him of individual responsibility.[3]

Hitchens charged that for someone else to take your punishment is deeply immoral.

But it is not just atheists who might raise questions about our understanding of Jesus dying in our place. As Christians, we might

1 For example, see his debate with Christian apologist John Lennox at the 2008 Edinburgh Festival, "Christopher Hitchens vs John Lennox: Can Atheism Save Europe? Debate," Larry Alex Taunton, filmed August 2008, posted March 28, 2017, YouTube video, 1:08:04, https://www.youtube.com/.

2 For one example, see Larry Alex Taunton, *The Faith of Christopher Hitchens: The Restless Soul of the World's Most Notorious Atheist* (Nashville: Thomas Nelson, 2017).

3 Christopher Hitchens, *Letters to a Young Contrarian* (New York: Basic Books, 2001), 58.

have our own quiet concerns. After all, the Bible itself condemns the idea of the innocent being punished and the guilty going free:

> He who justifies the wicked and he who condemns the
>   righteous
>   are both alike an abomination to the LORD. (Prov. 17:15)

"Abomination" is a strong word, referring to especially serious sins and violations of God's covenant. This is not just something God disapproves of; it offends the very core of his being.

It offends us too. Whenever we come across a miscarriage of justice, we feel deep revulsion. When we learn of someone falsely imprisoned or of a notorious criminal repeatedly escaping justice, we can't help but be deeply troubled. People should be treated with equity. Justice should be blind.

So what should we make of the death of Jesus? Is it not an example of the very thing this proverb condemns? After all, because of the cross of Christ, Paul can describe God as "him who justifies the ungodly" (Rom. 4:5). If that is who God is, then how can he be just? If that is what the cross brings about, then how should we feel about it? Are we not benefitting from an act of profound injustice? We might wonder whether Christopher Hitchens was right—whether this belief in Christ dying for us is itself immoral.

Justice at the Cross

The same Paul who describes God as justifying the ungodly also maintains that the death of Jesus was not only not unjust but the very clearest expression of God's righteousness. Far from being the place where we might question God's justice, it's actually where we most see his moral integrity. Speaking of Christ's death, he writes,

> This was to show God's righteousness, because in his divine forbearance he had passed over former sins. It was to show his righteousness at the present time, so that he might be just and the justifier of the one who has faith in Jesus. (Rom. 3:25–26)

Twice we're told that the cross was "to show God's righteousness," dealing with our sin "so that he might be just." Somehow, this very death of Jesus for us is the demonstration and proof of God's justice rather than the contradiction of it.

So how does this work? How can God justify the ungodly *and* demonstrate his own justice in doing so? Surely God can only either justify sinners *or* be just, right?

But Paul asserts both these things because he means to and because he believes both. At the cross, he explains, we ungodly souls are justified, but God does this in a way that proves him to be utterly just and righteous in doing so.

It is understanding our union with Christ that helps us see how this can be. Our being in Christ is what enables Jesus to take our place in such a way that is just and good. God can make us right with him and be right to do so. We can be justified *justly*.

It matters that we understand this idea. When someone helps us, even significantly, we feel deeply uneasy if we find out it has come by nefarious means.

In an episode of the political drama *The West Wing*, the president's chief of staff, Leo McGarry, is facing a crisis as details of his past stint in rehab have been leaked to his political opponents. In an effort to help him, two of his colleagues visit a call girl to see if she happens to have any dirt on these opponents. Leo finds out, and while he's touched by their concern for him, he's ultimately deeply unhappy with their underhand tactics. "It's not what we do," he tells them, and then repeats it slowly for emphasis: "*It's not what we do.*"[4]

Concerning the death of Jesus, we need to know that what he has done for us is something we can feel good about, that God has not compromised his moral goodness to share his love with us.

The Cross and Union with Christ

The first thing we must do is rule out a common misunderstanding about the nature of what Christ was doing for us on the cross.

A few years ago, a friend and I were visiting a city for a couple of days and went to a spy museum, where we learned how to be spies for the day. Both of us have enjoyed spy movies our whole lives, so we felt this was the moment to finally put all those hours of viewing to good use. The day started with some briefings, after which we would be let loose on the city to follow clues and foil some hypothetical terrorist plot. Needless to say, we were distracted during the briefings and eager to get out into "the field" to do our thing. Once out, we furtively crisscrossed the city, accumulated intelligence, stopped for multiple coffee breaks, succeeded in looking and feeling like spies, but manifestly failed to prevent the attack on the city (sorry, Washington, DC). But that didn't matter—we were *spies*.

One of the briefings I did pay attention to was on how to do a briefcase drop. This is where you surreptitiously leave a briefcase

4 *The West Wing*, season 1, episode 10, "In Excelsis Deo," directed by Alex Graves, written by Aaron Sorkin and Rick Cleveland, aired December 15, 1999, on NBC.

of intelligence somewhere for another person to come along and pick up a few moments later. We were told that it needed to be somewhere public but not too public. Park benches were recommended as the right kind of place. The first agent takes a seat at the bench, nonchalantly sets the briefcase down beside it, and then gets up a few moments later and walks off without it. The second agent then sits at the very same place for a moment or two before leaving with the case in hand. The point (we were told) was that it needs to be somewhere open (where you can come and go freely, blending in with the public) but not too busy (where someone else might pick up the case instead).

Now, I suspect briefcases are not the most essential piece of equipment in espionage and that the museum was catering more to our image of spying rather than the actual reality of it. But the point is this: it can be easy to think of the death of Jesus as being a bit like a briefcase drop. One party brings something and then leaves it for another person to collect and use.

In this case, Jesus dies and procures our salvation, and two thousand years later we turn up and (by faith) pick it up and take it home. It is all entirely impersonal, rather like collecting a package someone has mailed to a special mailbox for you. You collect the goods but never actually come into contact with the sender.

Some of the ways the cross is explained can unwittingly fuel this kind of misunderstanding. Sometimes the cross is spoken of in merely transactional terms: Christ provides our justification, we receive it, and we all go on our way. I've heard many talks suggesting that our sin is like a big book we carry in our hands that Jesus then takes and carries in his own. Or he puts on our "sin" T-shirt, and we put on his "righteousness" T-shirt. These illustrations communicate something true—Jesus voluntarily taking on himself what should have been ours and giving us what should have been his—but in a way that implies something of a relational distance between us, as if he is just an unrelated third party or some nameless agent.

Our union with Christ shows us that this could not be more wrong. It shows us that we are not independent parties involved in some remote transaction. He is not a benevolent stranger coming along to help us out. He has made us one with him and has done so in a particular way that underscores the rightness of what he is accomplishing for us. The category Scripture often uses to describe this kind of union is marriage. Jesus refers to himself not only as our Savior, Redeemer, and friend but also as a *bridegroom*. In fact, it is only by being so that he can be those other things to us as well.

Consider the following encounter from Mark's Gospel:

> And people came and said to him, "Why do John's disciples and the disciples of the Pharisees fast, but your disciples do not fast?" And Jesus said to them, "Can the wedding guests fast while the bridegroom is with them? As long as they have the bridegroom with them, they cannot fast. The days will come when the bridegroom is taken away from them, and then they will fast in that day." (Mark 2:18–20)

Jesus is being asked why his disciples are not fasting, and he answers by saying it would be like fasting at a wedding feast. There are many times when we might try to hold back on what we eat, but a wedding reception is not meant to be one of those times.

It is a celebration, and one of the ways we express celebration is by feasting together. This is not the time to count calories and turn away food that is brought to you. To do so could even be offensive to the happy couple.

Jesus is saying that this precious time his disciples have with him—soon to come to an abrupt and violent end—is just like being at a wedding feast. At this moment, the disciples are with the bridegroom; when he is taken from them, they will indeed fast.

John the Baptist also picks up on this idea, describing himself as the "friend of the bridegroom":

The friend of the bridegroom, who stands and hears him, rejoices greatly at the bridegroom's voice. Therefore this joy of mine is now complete. He must increase, but I must decrease. (John 3:29–30)

The role of a best man is significant and visible: he is at the groom's side; he might look after the rings until they're exchanged in the ceremony; he is expected to deliver a speech, giving the inside scoop on the groom and commending him to those present. The whole point of his visibility is to serve and make way for the groom— to give attention *to* him and not draw it away *from* him. This is how John the Baptist sees his ministry: he is there to make way for Jesus. Spiritually, he's the best man; Jesus is the bridegroom.

We see this same marital language throughout the New Testament:

"Therefore a man shall leave his father and mother and hold fast to his wife, and the two shall become one flesh." This mystery is profound, and I am saying that it refers to Christ and the church. (Eph. 5:31–32)

Or do you not know that he who is joined to a prostitute becomes one body with her? For, as it is written, "The two will become one flesh." But he who is joined to the Lord becomes one spirit with him. (1 Cor. 6:16–17)

Let us rejoice and exult
    and give him the glory,
for the marriage of the Lamb has come,
    and his Bride has made herself ready. (Rev. 19:7)

And I saw the holy city, new Jerusalem, coming down out of heaven from God, prepared as a bride adorned for her husband. And I heard a loud voice from the throne saying, "Behold, the dwelling place of God is with man. He will dwell with them, and they will be his people, and God himself will be with them as their God." (Rev. 21:2–3)

So the idea that the church's relationship to Jesus is a marriage relationship is not incidental to the Bible. It is one of the primary categories Scripture has for it.[5]

This has many implications, of course. But one of the most significant is this: in a marital union, *it is entirely proper for the property of one to become the property of the other*. It is proper in

---

5   For a wonderful treatment of this theme across the whole Bible, see Ray Ortlund, *Marriage and the Mystery of the Gospel*, Short Studies in Biblical Theology (Wheaton, IL: Crossway, 2016).

the marital union of a husband and wife; it is also proper in the supraunion of Jesus and his people. What is his becomes ours, and what is ours becomes his.

As a pastor, I get to officiate weddings from time to time. One of the more recent was when I married a man who was a *Star Trek* fan to a woman who was a Justin Bieber fan. As we ran through the vows, they each said the words "All that I have, I give to you." In marriage, you don't just get the person; you get what he or she comes with. Like it or not, this bride could not have this man without also having his *Star Trek* costumes. He could not have this bride without also having all her Justin Bieber memorabilia. Such is the nature of marriage. The estate of the one rightly becomes the estate of the other. The marriage vows say, in effect and among other things, "What's mine is now yours."

When we come to Jesus, we enter into this kind of union with him. What naturally belongs to Jesus becomes ours. And what naturally belongs to us becomes his. That is what it means to be one with him. We receive what is properly his, and he receives what is properly ours. It is the fruit of our union. Michael Reeves puts it like this: "Christians don't imagine Jesus somehow floating his righteousness to us through space and time. We are clothed in his righteousness because we really are *in him*."[6] He continues:

> That is the great marriage swap, or joyful exchange, of the gospel. Christ, our great Bridegroom, has taken all our sin, death, and judgement, borne it on the cross, and drowned

---

6   Michael Reeves, *Right with God* (Bridgend, UK: Union, 2022), 26.

it in his blood. He has then given to us all his righteousness, blessedness, and beloved status before his Father. Because of this, said Luther, the sinner can confidently display "her sins in the face of death and hell and say, 'If I have sinned, yet my Christ, in whom I believe, has not sinned, and all his is mine and all mine is his.' "[7]

Christ can therefore take on himself our condemnation and credit us with his righteousness.

God's Righteousness Displayed

This glorious reality is expressed in one of the most significant verses in all the Bible:

> For our sake he made him to be sin who knew no sin, so that in him we might become the righteousness of God. (2 Cor. 5:21)

Paul outlines what has happened at the cross.

Christ had no sin of his own but at the cross took on himself all of ours. He was "made . . . to be sin" not in the sense of being in any way sinful himself but in the sense of being so identified with all the accumulated sins of all his people. Correspondingly, his righteousness—the righteousness of God—is reckoned to us such that we in turn "become" it, declared righteous before God. This is *justification*: receiving now, through the finished work of Christ on the cross, God's verdict that we have a righteous status before him.

---

7   Reeves, *Right with God*, 32.

When I was in high school, it was common to be given a question on exams asking you to "justify your answer." Maybe it was a history exam and the question was about how regressive the reign of Henry VII was or about which factors were most determining in the run-up to the First World War. Whatever answer you gave, you had to justify it—you had to show it to be in the right. Through the death of Jesus, God is able to declare that we are in the right with him.

Dane Ortlund sums up the wonder of all this:

> Here we penetrate into the core difference between Christianity and every other world religion. We become acceptable and beautiful before God not by what we bring but by what Christ brings, not by what we do but by what he has done. In a wondrous interchange God legally imputes to us Christ's righteous record and imputes to Christ our wretched record (cf. 1 Cor. 1:30). He, the billionaire, takes our unpayable debt; we, the beggar, receive his bottomless fortune.[8]

We are justified in Christ. No pretense is involved. No trickery. God has not had to close his eyes to the reality of what we're like. Nor has he had to compromise his standards. He shows us unfathomable mercy, in no way at the expense of his perfect justice.

This is why Paul can say that the cross is a *demonstration* of God's justice. Far from being immoral in the way Christopher

---

8   Dane Ortlund, *2 Corinthians*, in *Romans–Galatians*, vol. 10 of *ESV Expository Commentary*, ed. Iain M. Duguid, James M. Hamilton Jr., and Jay Sklar (Wheaton, IL: Crossway, 2020), 477.

Hitchens imagined, the cross is where we most clearly see God's righteousness:

> This was to show God's righteousness, because in his divine forbearance he had passed over former sins. It was to show his righteousness at the present time, so that he might be just and the justifier of the one who has faith in Jesus. (Rom. 3:25–26)

Paul is anticipating a particular reason someone might think God is unjust: "He had passed over former sins" (Rom. 3:25).

Over the course of history, so the objection goes, there has been an apparent lack of divine justice. The wicked have acted with impunity while receiving no visible judgment from heaven. God has not stepped in. An ever-increasing backlog of unpunished sin has been building up over the centuries. Perhaps God does not ultimately care.

The cross of Christ is the definitive answer to this charge. Paul shows us that those sins had gone unpunished not because of God's indifference to justice but because of his *mercy to the unjust*. It was because of his "divine forbearance" (Rom. 3:25). He wasn't forgoing his judgment; he was postponing it—postponing it in his kindness. Sins that had been unpunished were now being fully dealt with at the cross. When Jesus cried out, "My God, my God, why have you forsaken me?" (Mark 15:34), we saw God's commitment to executing justice. The full horror of what Jesus experienced in his crucifixion was not just physical (unimaginable though that is for so many of us) but spiritual. He was experiencing the condemnation we deserved. He who "knew no sin" was "made . . . to be sin" for our sakes

(2 Cor. 5:21). No one can properly look at the death of Jesus and think that God is indifferent to sin. The cross demonstrates God's righteousness.

So Paul can say that God "might be just and the justifier of the one who has faith in Jesus" (Rom. 3:26). In other words, God can justify us *and* be just in doing so. He can make *us* right in a way that *is* right. The ungodly can be declared righteous with no foul play involved. God expresses his mercy *and* underscores his moral integrity. We can marvel at his love *and* justice. The cross shows us "God's righteous way of righteoussing the unrighteous."[9]

Humility

At least two things flow from this teaching. The first Paul gets to immediately—humility:

> Then what becomes of our boasting? It is excluded. By what kind of law? By a law of works? No, but by the law of faith. (Rom. 3:27)

The very first effect of truly understanding how we're justified in Christ is the removal of boasting. Paul is emphatic: "It is excluded." It cannot coexist with a true grasp of what Jesus has done for us. The reason is simple: we are saved by faith in Christ. I have contributed nothing to my salvation other than my colossal need for it. I can point to nothing in myself for my justification. There is no ground for boasting in myself. All I have done is receive in my empty hands of faith all that Christ has done for me. It is all

9   John R. W. Stott, *The Cross of Christ* (London: Inter-Varsity Press, 1986), 244.

of him and nothing of myself. He didn't meet me halfway. This wasn't a matching grant. He did it all.

When I initially arrived at university, the first few weeks of conversations were dominated by where we all came from and what grades we had gotten to earn admittance to a particular program. Everyone there had earned their place, of course. The question was now simply finding out exactly how much each person had achieved academically.

There will be no such conversations in heaven. No person will enter heaven on the basis of what he or she has done. All of us will enjoy the happy awareness that we are there only by the merits of Jesus. We won't be boasting in ourselves. No one will care what grades I earned in high school or what kind of degree I got at university or how many friends I had or how much money I made or any of the other things we pin to ourselves as forms of validation.

Imagine if someone asked, "Why are *you* a Christian? How did *you* end up in a relationship with God?"

The only true answer is "Because of Jesus." It wasn't our wits, our spiritual awareness, our moral superiority, our religious accomplishments, our impeccable values, or our charitable endeavors. It was Jesus. There is no other reason we're here. All that we have, we have through him and by his grace.

Assurance

The second thing to flow from understanding how we're justified in Christ is therefore assurance.

Paul has made it clear that the cross was not God compromising his righteousness for the sake of showing us mercy. No, the cross is the ultimate demonstration of his mercy and his justice.

Neither is advanced at the cost of the other. God never has to switch between being gracious and being upright. The two are not opposite ends of a seesaw, one only rising if the other falls.

The cross is not unjust. God is not doing anything untoward by extending forgiveness to us when we come to him on the basis of what Jesus has done. This is seen clearly in these well-known words from John:

> If we say we have no sin, we deceive ourselves, and the truth is not in us. If we confess our sins, he is faithful and just to forgive us our sins and to cleanse us from all unrighteousness. (1 John 1:8–9)

There are only two alternatives: to *deny* our sin or to *confess* it. Simply being *without* it in the first place just isn't an option. We have it, and we either live in denial about it or come clean about it.

John shows us what will happen when we do the latter. God does two things: he forgives us, and he cleanses us. We need both. We need to be *forgiven*—for all that we have done not to count against us, for our track record to be expunged. We also need to be *cleansed*. Sinning is not just what I have been doing, it is (apart from God) who I am and part of my nature. So simply being forgiven what I have done won't stop me from going on to do it again. I also need to be cleansed in my nature. My actions need to be forgiven, *and* I need to be changed into someone who won't keep living to do those very things.

God can do these two things for us, John says, because he *is* two things: "He is faithful and just."

We expect to see the word "faithful" here. God is being faithful when he forgives and cleanses us because that is what he said he would do to all who come to him in the name of Christ. He is being as good as his word. He is keeping his promises. He is being faithful.

But John says he is also being "just." God is just when he forgives those who confess their sins. He is not turning a blind eye to their transgressions; those very sins are condemned:

> For God has done what the law, weakened by the flesh, could not do. By sending his own Son in the likeness of sinful flesh and for sin, he condemned sin in the flesh. (Rom. 8:3)

The cross, more than anything else, shows us just how seriously God takes our sin. Sin is fully dealt with there so that we can be justly forgiven and cleansed.

John Piper goes even further:

> This text says God would be *unjust* (not merely unmerciful) not to forgive us if we confess our sins. Why is that? Why is forgiveness now a matter of justice and not merely a matter of mercy? The answer is that Jesus has shed his blood (1 John 1:7) to make a just recompense for all who confess their sins and take refuge in him. This God would be unjust not to forgive them, *not* because they have honored him by their sinless lives, but because they take refuge in the name of Jesus. The death of Jesus so honored the Father and so vindicated the glory of his name that God is bound by his justice, not just his mercy, to forgive all who stake their lives on the worth of Jesus.[10]

10 John Piper, *The Pleasures of God*, in *The Collected Works of John Piper* (Wheaton, IL: Crossway, 2017), 2:539.

The cross is where God has most clearly revealed himself. It is where we most vividly see his mercy and his justice, his love and his wrath, his grace and his truth. These things all come together in the death of Jesus. There is no tension between them.

I began this chapter by talking about a very powerful experience in Cuba, among a group of men freshly reveling in the mercies of God at the cross of Christ. I have never seen anything like it. On the flight home, my plane ran into some of the severest turbulence I've ever experienced. We were being bounced around the billowing clouds like a pinball. I really felt like we might fall out of the sky at any moment. But I didn't feel anxious about that. I was having my own high-altitude Nunc Dimittis, ready to depart this world given what I had just seen. With these other men, it was as though we were all at the foot of the cross.

When they had sung of the wonder and beauty of the cross, many with eyes squeezed shut and tears shining on their cheeks, they hadn't been wasting their breath. They hadn't been celebrating an injustice or, to return to Christopher Hitchens's charge, something that was morally repugnant. Salvation is not like sausage meat, only enjoyable to experience if you don't find out where it came from. No, we can feel good about what God has done for us. And God can be pleased with it too. And all because we are in Christ!

5

New in Christ

Therefore, if anyone is in Christ, he is a new creation.
The old has passed away; behold, the new has come.

2 CORINTHIANS 5:17

THE TERM MIGHT NOT be familiar to you, but the concept behind it most likely is—*imposter syndrome*. It's the feeling, often experienced in professional or academic contexts, that you can't really do what everyone believes you can and expects of you. You feel like an imposter. Any success you seem to have experienced up until this point was a fluke. You're a fraud, and any moment now everyone is going to realize it. It's only a matter of time.

Maybe you've felt like this in the workplace or at a school. I just experienced it today, the day I am writing this chapter. I've been speaking at a conference where all the other speakers are people I deeply admire, people who are unusually gifted and able, people you would expect to be at these sorts of events. So what was *I* doing there? Surely there must have been some mistake. The moment I step up to the podium, it will be obvious to all—*I don't belong here.*

In the very early days of Facebook, I was involved with college ministry at the University of Oxford, and I recall a group appearing on it at the start of the new academic year called "I Got into Oxford by Mistake: Can I Go Home Now Please?" It almost immediately numbered several hundred members. For some it would have been a bit of a joke. But many of the students I was talking to were very serious. They felt profoundly out of their depth.

But the existence of such a group was also a comfort. If so many others are feeling like imposters, then you realize you're not on your own and slowly start to feel like less of an imposter. Part of how this syndrome works is that you assume that everyone else is fitting in just fine and that only you have a problem.

Spiritual Imposters?

It is very easy for Christians to experience a form of imposter syndrome. As we look around at the other people at church, it can seem as though they all belong here. They seem to have the Christian life figured out. They seem to know what they're doing. But it is a different story for ourselves. We might have been a Christian for years, but it still feels as though it hasn't really taken yet. We want to be real Christians but wonder if we ever will be. It doesn't seem to come very naturally to us; we're still far from figuring it all out.

We can feel this most intently with *holiness*. We know it is commanded of us. We certainly want to live in a way that's worthy of the gospel. We want to change, to be more like Jesus. Yet it can feel so alien to us. Even the word *holy* sounds somewhat otherworldly. Our default settings seem to take us in the opposite direction. Whatever holiness is, it isn't me. It's like trying to speak in an unfamiliar language or like trying on clothes that don't quite fit. We wonder if there is any point in persisting with it. Why try to be someone you're clearly not? And so when we're around other believers who seem to be living the Christian life with an approximation of success, we feel like the odd one out. An imposter.

It is a very understandable way to feel. But we need to remember two things: (1) way more people are feeling the very same way, and (2) we're comparing what's happening on the inside of our lives with what's happening on the outside of theirs, which is hardly a fair fight. It's the difference between having a front-row seat at a movie theater versus trying to listen in from the outside with your head pressed up against the wall. Our own heart is on view to us twenty-four seven in high definition. No one else's is. So when we're tempted to look at other believers, wondering how they seem to have cracked the Christian life so effortlessly, we need to bear in mind that others are probably looking at us in the same way.

Rethinking Sin

But natural though it might seem to think this way, it is actually completely untrue. The Bible is, of course, deeply realistic about the continuing presence of sinful tendencies in our lives. We are not yet rid of our sinful nature. The apostle John shows us that to think otherwise is a serious mistake:

If we say we have no sin, we deceive ourselves, and the truth is not in us. . . . If we say we have not sinned, we make him a liar, and his word is not in us. (1 John 1:8, 10)

We can't deny the reality of sin in our lives. To claim that we haven't sinned or that sin isn't within our nature in any way is to lie to ourselves while calling God a liar. Foundational to healthy Christianity is coming to terms with our sin. Even the most mature and "advanced" disciples are not done with sin. In this life, our sin will never be fully in the rearview mirror. It will always be something we have to reckon with.

But that is not all there is to say on this matter. If one mistake is to claim that our faith in Christ means we're effectively done with sin, another is to fail to grasp just how radically different things are now that Jesus is in our lives.

It's easy to think of the Christian life as being like that scene from the classic action movie *Raiders of the Lost Ark*, where Indiana Jones manages to leap onto the side of the Nazis' truck, proceeds to climb in through the side door and throw a startled passenger out onto the road, and then wrestles the driver in an attempt to get control of the truck. As they fight, the truck veers and lurches about.

It's a common trope in action movies—the hero and villain fighting each other for control of the vehicle/plane/spaceship at a key moment in the story. And it feels a lot like what is going on inside of us as Christians. Christ has come to us and is now fighting our sinful nature. On our worse days, we wonder if he will prevail.

But the wonderful news of the gospel is that my relationship to sin has now radically changed. Yes, sin is still kicking around in my heart, but I relate to it in a fundamentally different way now. The reason? *Who I am* is fundamentally different:

> It is no longer I who live, but Christ who lives in me. The life I now live in the flesh I live by faith in the Son of God, who loved me and gave himself for me. (Gal. 2:20)

It is true that a battle is going on inside us—a battle between what Paul calls the desires of the flesh and the desires of the Spirit (Gal. 5:17). But we mustn't miss the larger point Paul has been making: "It is no longer I who live, but Christ who lives in me." This gets us to the heart of something central to the Bible's teaching on what it means to be a Christian. Our union with Christ doesn't just mean that he identifies with us (wonderful though that is). It also means we identify with him—in a "this changes everything" kind of way. Our union means that we identify with him in his death and rising. We died with him, and we have new life in him. Both are fundamental to understanding how and why knowing Jesus truly transforms us.

In Christ We Have Died

Paul is saying that, in one sense, coming to Christ means we actually die: "I no longer live." A death has taken place. The "I" that had existed—living apart from Christ and oblivious to spiritual realities—that "I" has now died and been replaced by another "I": Christ in me. And so the life Paul now lives is grounded in a fundamentally different reality: "I live by faith in the Son of God, who loved me and gave himself for me" (Gal. 2:20). The death of Christ for us does not merely add a new dimension to our existing lives; it completely reshapes and redefines them, so much so that Paul can consider the old life to have died.

Paul makes a similar point to his readers in Rome. Having explained how Christians are justified by faith and how Christ's work on the cross can reverse Adam's sin, he anticipates a likely question:

> What shall we say then? Are we to continue in sin that grace may abound? By no means! How can we who died to sin still live in it? (Rom. 6:1–2)

We might ask this question in two ways. There is the mischievous way. Having learned from Paul that "where sin increased, grace abounded all the more" (Rom. 5:20), we might think that this is license to keep on sinning. If the death of Christ is more than sufficient for all my sin, then isn't that a blank check to just carry on sinning, assured that all of it will be covered? If you're forgiven for free, why not continue offending?

The second way of asking might be more likely for many of us. It rises out of not mischief but despair. Think of it this way: God is able to bring glory to himself by saving undeserving and helpless sinners like us. In fact, God shows his glory precisely in how our sin is no match for Christ's death. The shocking extent of our sin is nothing compared to the extraordinary extent of Jesus's grace. So has God set this up in such a way that I am *meant* to continue in sin so that he can continue to be glorified for providing ongoing grace for it?

One form of the question thus arises from a *desire* to keep on sinning, the other from a fear that we might *have* to. The answer to both is the same: a resounding and unequivocal *no*. "By no means!" Absolutely not. No way. His short answer: we've died to sin, so we can't still live in it.

Now for the longer answer:

> Do you not know that all of us who have been baptized into Christ Jesus were baptized into his death? We were buried therefore with him by baptism into death, in order that, just as Christ was raised from the dead by the glory of the Father, we too might walk in newness of life. (Rom. 6:3–4)

Death always means finality. When we talk about a joke dying, we mean that the laughter never materialized, and we'll never try that one again. When we talk about an idea or a dream dying, we mean it is gone forever. Death is such a definitive ending.

Paul is showing us that our union with Christ—spoken of in the language of baptism—is a union with his death. Paul underscores the reality of our death with Christ in the strongest possible language:

> We know that our old self was crucified with him in order that the body of sin might be brought to nothing, so that we would no longer be enslaved to sin. (Rom. 6:6)

Paul is emphatic: the old self has died. God didn't enter into negotiation with it. He didn't try to reason with it. He didn't even just yell at it. It has been crucified.

This shows us something of the severity of our situation. This, and nothing less than this, is what needed to happen to us.

One of the ironies of my working life is that my very first paid job was as a gardener. Each Saturday morning I would head across the neighborhood to the home of a somewhat crotchety old man we called "the Major," where I would help work in his garden for a few hours. It wasn't a happy arrangement. I have no natural aptitude for this sort of thing; he wasn't willing to pay more than the equivalent of three dollars an hour. His money didn't seem worth it to me, and my work certainly wasn't worth it to him. So when, many years later, I had a problem with an overgrown hedge threatening to pull down the wooden fence it had been planted next to, I knew I was going to need someone else's help with it. As it happened, a couple of friends said they would come over one day while I was at work and sort it out for me. I got home that day expecting to see a hedge that looked neatly trimmed. What I discovered was that it had gone. My friends explained to me that it didn't need to be cut back; it needed to be totally removed.

This is true of our old self. It didn't need a slap on the wrist. It didn't need to be *improved*. It needed to be *killed*. And so it had to be "crucified with him."

This is important to note. It is common to think of what Christ has done as simply being the means by which I can avoid death. He died the death I deserve so that I don't ever have to. That is not untrue, of course. Christ experienced the godforsakenness that should have been mine and that my sin fully deserved. I will now, wonderfully, never have to face that. But I actually need Jesus to do two things for me on the cross: to take the consequences of all my sin and to deal with the sinful nature that got me into this mess to start with. If he just dealt with the former, I would have assurance of forgiveness but no actual hope of changing. I would keep living in the same sinful, self-destructive patterns. I need Jesus to help me not just with the penalty of my sin but with the very root of it inside of me. And so, as Paul says, on that same cross my sinful nature—the old self—was crucified with Christ. Jesus did not die so that I could go on living as I was in a sinful state; he died so that my sin nature could die with him. The old life has come to an end.

In Christ We Are Raised to New Life

The old self has died with Christ, and yet I still live. I have *new life* in him. Christ is in me, and my life is now defined by him and what he has done rather than by me and my own sinful agenda.

This is why Paul can also say, "Therefore, if anyone is in Christ, he is a new creation. The old has passed away; behold, the new has come" (2 Cor. 5:17). Jesus has not just enhanced us but *remade* us. There has not just been a change *in* me; there has been a change *of* me. It is not just my life that is different; *I* am different. And that means we now have a new relationship to sin:

> Now if we have died with Christ, we believe that we will also live with him. We know that Christ, being raised from the dead, will never die again; death no longer has dominion over him. For the death he died he died to sin, once for all, but the life he lives he lives to God. So you also must consider yourselves dead to sin and alive to God in Christ Jesus. (Rom. 6:8–11)

Here we have the same logic: "We have died." This time Paul adds "with Christ." This is how we can die and yet still live. Our union with Christ is a union with his death and resurrection. It might look like I was born two thousand years too late and on the wrong continent to have been around for the events of that first Good Friday and Easter Sunday, but through my union with him, there is a sense in which I was *there*. I died with him in his death and can now live with him in his life.

Paul shows us the kind of death Christ died (and to which I am therefore united): *a death to sin*. So those of us in him must now think of ourselves as also being dead to sin. Our relationship to sin has thus been irrevocably changed.

"Consider yourselves dead to sin" (Rom. 6:11) is the first imperative to come in the letter to the Romans, and it concerns how we *think*. Paul does not say, "*Be* dead to sin," as if we could somehow make ourselves completely unresponsive to sin. Paul says, "*Consider* yourselves dead to sin." The key is our understanding. We are now to think about ourselves in a new way.

Paul shows us what this new thinking involves: "For sin will have no dominion over you, since you are not under law but under grace" (Rom. 6:14).

Sin's dominion over us had been obvious. Jesus himself said, "Everyone who practices sin is a slave to sin" (John 8:34). Our propensity to sin is not just an unavoidable habit; it is a form of bondage. By nature, we can't release ourselves from sin.

The nature of our slavery has now radically changed. We are now bound to Jesus's death to sin, and so sin is no longer our master. That does not mean it exerts no influence over us; it means it has no authority over us. We never have to do what it says. That doesn't mean we won't ever sin; it does mean that every time we do, we didn't have to.

This is why Paul urges us to consider ourselves dead to sin. When we are used to obeying a particular voice, it is hard to stop doing so even when we no longer have to. A few years after I finished high school, I was invited back to speak briefly at one of the daily student assemblies—they often had former students back to share what they were now up to. As I walked up the familiar street to the school entrance, I realized how *small* the students now seemed to me. Compared to them, I felt like a man of the world. I was several years older than these kids. I had gone through university and started full-time work. But when we walked into the hall where the school assemblies took place, I suddenly felt like I was fifteen again. The hall hadn't changed. The musty smell lingered. The wooden chairs creaked. There was still the same headmaster as when I had been there, still looking much the same. It suddenly felt as if no time had passed at all.[1]

As he was giving the announcements, the headmaster suddenly shouted, "Sit up straight!" Instinctively, I corrected my posture and sat bolt upright. Then I realized he was talking not to me but to someone else. And *then* it hit me: he wasn't my headmaster anymore. I didn't have to do what he said. He had no authority over me. But many years of having to obey him meant I still had a reflex to do so. I had to make an effort *not* to.

It is the same with sin. For so many years, we were under its sway. We marched to its beat. We sinned at an instinctive, intuitive level. We didn't really have to think about it. It came so naturally. But that has now changed. Sin no longer has authority

---

1   This analogy is adapted from Sam Allberry, *Lifted: Experiencing the Resurrection Life* (Nottingham, UK: Inter-Varsity Press, 2010), 70.

over me. I'm not bound to it and am under no obligation to it. That doesn't mean I don't ever sin. But it does mean that every time I do, I don't *have* to. I never *have* to sin. There is always an alternative.

Knowing this is a great help in fighting sin. Each of us will have many sins of which we are particularly conscious. There will be others we are barely aware of. David could therefore pray,

> Who can discern his errors?
> Declare me innocent from hidden faults. (Ps. 19:12)

But most of us will have particular besetting sins that seem so established, we can't imagine them ever going away. It is all we've ever known. This is who we've always been. So when temptation comes, it often says to us, "This is who you are. This is how we roll. Stop pretending to be something you're not." It can sound compelling, and we can easily just give up. The *real* me is the me who keeps doing this particular sin.

If that is our mindset, we can see why it is hard to think anything will ever change. These besetting sins appear so deeply baked into who we are that it's hard to think of a me that doesn't do them. The sin has become defining. Pursuing holiness is trying to be a version of me I'll never actually be.

This is why our union with Christ is so wonderfully empowering. Yes, that sin may well have been something that defined my life—maybe for many, many years. Perhaps it really was who *I* really was. But even if so, my union with Christ means *it is no longer who I am*. In Christ, *I* am now different, *I* have changed, *I* have been made new.

This is the point Paul has to remind his Corinthian readers of:

> Or do you not know that the unrighteous will not inherit the kingdom of God? Do not be deceived: neither the sexually immoral, nor idolaters, nor adulterers, nor men who practice homosexuality, nor thieves, nor the greedy, nor drunkards, nor revilers, nor swindlers will inherit the kingdom of God. And such were some of you. But you were washed, you were sanctified, you were justified in the name of the Lord Jesus Christ and by the Spirit of our God. (1 Cor. 6:9–11)

Look at what has changed. There were once people in Corinth who could be described as "the sexually immoral" or "the greedy" or "drunkards" or "swindlers." That was who they were. Those sins defined them. Being a drunkard (for example) was not just something they did; it was who they were. But now these very same people have been transformed. They are now followers of Christ and part of the church in Corinth. So Paul can say, "Such *were* some of you." Yes, that is who you *were*, but it is no longer who you *are*. You have changed. What has accounted for this shift? "You were washed, you were sanctified, you were justified in the name of our Lord Jesus Christ and by the Spirit of our God."

This is the transformation that has taken place in the life of every Christian believer. Coming to Christ means not just a new set of aspirations and intentions. It means a new nature, a new heart, a new spirit within us. Being washed, sanctified, and justified in Jesus and by his Spirit utterly redefines who we are. So whatever sin seemed most to characterize your past no longer defines your present. Whatever you once were, you no longer are. The change wrought by Christ is that definitive.

Paul is needing to spell this out to the Corinthians precisely because it is not obvious to them. He would not need to warn them that the unrighteous would not inherit the kingdom of God were it not for the fact that they are being tempted in some way to go back into that unrighteousness. And the most powerful argument to deter them from doing so is to remind them that this is not who they are anymore.

We can see how this can help us in our own fight against particularly besetting sins. When the New Testament calls us to holiness, it is calling us to be who we *now* are. If I am who I am in Christ, then it is *holiness*—not sinfulness—that is now who I most truly am in the deepest core of my being. However deep sinful feelings may go, the new love and life we have in Christ goes deeper still. It is sin—rather than living for Christ—that now goes against the grain of my true self. Pursuing him is the most true to myself I can ever be.

So think about the sin that seems most besetting in your life. It might have shaped your behavior many years. It might still exert a powerful gravitational pull on your heart. But if so, *it is not who you are.* Indulging such feelings is never being true to yourself as the person you now are in Christ. What is most true of any of us as believers is never going to be an aspect of our sinful nature. If we get this backward, we will not feel we have the power to live like Christ. It is why it is so profoundly unwise to define ourselves by any one of our sins, even while trying to fight them. If you're resisting something all the while believing it is who you *really* are, it will be that much harder to imagine any kind of victory over it. Confessing sin is one thing—the Bible calls us to confess to God as well as to one another. But there is a difference between confessing sin and identifying by it. To attempt Christian living with an un-Christian form of self-understanding produces a very unstable compound, and the danger is that eventually you will end up conforming your lifestyle to your identity. Who we think "we really are" has a profoundly powerful effect on how we expect to be able to live. Knowing who we really are through our union with Christ makes all the difference.

Union with Christ means that, ultimately, sin is the real imposter in our lives.

6

Holy in Christ

No one who abides in [Christ] keeps on sinning.

1 JOHN 3:6

SOME FRIENDS OF MINE recently completed the process of adopting a beautiful little girl. She had previously been in foster care for a number of years, and, needless to say, the idea of being with a new family on a permanent basis has led to some issues with her. Over the years, she had developed some patterns of behavior that seemed to stem from being moved from one house to another—coping mechanisms, of a sort, for all the temporariness and lack of ongoing emotional commitment. Her behavior had certainly proved challenging for her new parents, but the child psychologist assured them that it was to be expected as she made the adjustment to an entirely new way of living and that over time things should settle down a bit. Such is the complexity of finding a forever home for the first time.

To be united to Christ is to *abide* in him. Our coming to Christ is not a temporary expedient, like ducking under a tree for a few minutes to avoid some rain. We have found ourselves in a "forever home," now part of a new spiritual family in Christ, sharing the blessings of knowing his Father and of being his cherished children. John says as much in his first letter:

> See what kind of love the Father has given to us, that we should be called children of God; and so we are. (1 John 3:1)

To be children of God is the product of lavish, heavenly love. We can barely get our heads around it. John seems to anticipate our disbelief by adding "and so we are." This is not just what we're *called*; it's what we *are*. It stretches belief that God would give his very best to those who deserve it the very least. It will take the rest of our lives for it to truly sink in.

Also, like my friends' new daughter, it will take time for us to adjust to our new reality. Patterns of behavior from our past life will continue to have something of a hold on us, making us lash out in ways that contradict our new and better circumstances. John anticipates this too with these stark and uncomfortable words: "No one who abides in [Christ] keeps on sinning" (1 John 3:6).

At first glance, it would be very easy to misunderstand what John is saying and to think that being a Christian means we no longer sin at all. Some have thought this at various points over the years, believing themselves to have attained some level of full spiritual obedience. The problems with this thinking are not hard to spot. For one, the Bible always assumes that we retain the capacity to sin and that we will sadly break God's law from time to time. To believe we can live without sin is a serious form of denial, as John himself points out just a few paragraphs earlier: "If we say we have no sin, we deceive ourselves, and the truth is not in us" (1 John 1:8). But of course, the more obvious problem with such a view is that it is very hard to make anyone close to us seriously believe we don't sin. I meet with a couple of Christian friends to confess sins and failings, and I sometimes think they would probably get a more comprehensive account of my failings if they asked my housemate rather than me. Which means that, for the vast majority of us, we read the words "No one who abides in [Christ] keeps on sinning" with quiet despair rather than settled presumption.

But if John is not saying that Christians no longer have the capacity to sin, what is he saying? Just this: that *being in Christ is the key to holiness.*

Union with Christ and Holiness

We've already seen that our union with Christ means that we are justified and made new. We have a new relationship to sin; it no longer has the hold over us it once had. We are not bound to it in the same way. We don't have to look at the worst traits within us and worry that things will never get better. The newness Jesus brings to us utterly transforms us. If it was true that before we were in Christ no area of life was what it should have been, then we also need to know that following him means no area will be what it would have been. Every part of life is affected by union with Christ. The entire trajectory of our life has been radically altered. Things are now moving in an entirely different direction. Sin is not part of God's agenda for our future with him. John is not saying that sin is impossible; he is saying it should now be *unthinkable*.

It is our union with Christ that brings this theme into sharp focus. It is precisely because we abide in Christ that Christians will not keep on sinning.

The immediate context of this verse sheds essential light on this matter:

> Everyone who makes a practice of sinning also practices lawlessness; sin is lawlessness. You know that he appeared in order to take away sins, and in him there is no sin. No one who abides in him keeps on sinning; no one who keeps on sinning has either seen him or known him. (1 John 3:4–6)

We can see the logic of these verses. John is showing us that the nature of sin is lawlessness. When we sin, we are not just rejecting God's ways; we're also rejecting his right to make demands of us. This then puts the purpose of Jesus's coming into sharp relief. Because sin is a rejection of God's rule, it needs to be taken away. We can't go on living in God's universe in open defiance of him; he can't go on reigning without dealing definitively with sin. So Jesus appeared. It had to be him because "in him there is no sin." If he was mired in his own sin, he would not be able to help us with ours. Only one without sin could bring us to freedom from it.

Jesus coming into the world was no small thing. He had to be coded into human DNA, to gestate in a womb, to be born and weaned, and to slowly grow into boyhood, young adulthood, and mature manhood over the course of many years. He tasted the limitations of human life: hunger, thirst, and weariness. He was exposed to the ravages of our broken world, experiencing distress, grief, and anger. He faced the force of human sin—of injustice, betrayal, abandonment, torture, humiliation, and ultimately death. Yet he did it all *to take away sins*. That was always the plan. This is what Christmas was for.

And this is the Christ in whom we now abide. We are one with him, forever united to him. We depend on him, we look to him, and we cherish him. In that light, why would we continue in the very thing he came, at such cost, to bring to an end? Why would we ever want to reinstate what he came to take away? Why would we attempt to rebuild what Jesus came to destroy? Why would we pull in the exact opposite direction of the one with whom we are in such loving union? Being united to him means being united to the purpose of his coming, to his purpose in dying.

Our union with Christ connects us to the purpose of his first coming. It also connects us to his second coming—and this too is reason to pursue holiness. Let's look again at those opening words from 1 John 3:

> See what kind of love the Father has given to us, that we should be called children of God; and so we are. The reason why the world does not know us is that it did not know him. Beloved, we are God's children now, and what we will be has not yet appeared; but we know that when he appears we shall be like him, because we shall see him as he is. And everyone who thus hopes in him purifies himself as he is pure. (1 John 3:1–3)

The Christ who came will one day appear. When he does, we will be transformed into his likeness. That is the mouth-watering prospect that awaits us.

So just as our life is now in Christ, so too is our hope. We hope "in him." Our union gives us a future. We are hidden with him now; our future has not yet been publicly disclosed. But we will one day be fully like him, and nothing could matter more. Of all the things that excite us about the age to come—enjoying resurrected bodies in a new creation, no more sickness and sorrow—supreme is the prospect that we will finally be not only *with* Jesus but *like* him.

And that hope drives our desire to be done with sin: "Everyone who thus hopes in him purifies himself as he is pure" (1 John 3:3). If our future is being like Jesus, our present is wanting to press toward that as much as we can. We want to be now what we know we will be then. If the future is Christlikeness, we want to strain toward that now.

Several years ago, some friends of mine were preparing to leave their home in Scotland to serve as missionaries in Cambodia. I went to visit them a few weeks before they were due to depart. To my surprise, they were already many months into language study. They wanted to get as far ahead as they could. They had also adjusted their diet in light of what they would be eating in Cambodia, cutting out foods they wouldn't have access to there. My thinking was *Why not make the most of those things while you still can?* Their thinking was *Let's do as much as we can now to adjust to how we will be then.* They wanted to make the transition as smooth as possible.

The same rationale is found in this passage. Knowing what we will be motivates us to adjust to that future reality now. Jesus is pure. We will be too when we become like him. So given that hope, we purify ourselves now. We want to reduce the culture shock when we get to heaven. Being in him is a wonderful motivation to be pure.

The View from Corinth

Paul makes a similar point to the church in Corinth:

> "All things are lawful for me," but not all things are helpful. "All things are lawful for me," but I will not be dominated by anything. "Food is meant for the stomach and the stomach for food"—and God will destroy both one and the other. The body is not meant for sexual immorality, but for the Lord, and the Lord for the body. And God raised the Lord and will also raise us up by his power. Do you not know that your bodies are members of Christ? Shall I then take the members of Christ and make them members of a prostitute? Never! Or do you not know that he who is joined to a prostitute becomes one body with her? For, as it is written, "The two will become one flesh." But he who is joined to the Lord becomes one spirit with him. Flee from sexual immorality. (1 Cor. 6:12–18)

The church in Corinth was, to use a pastoral euphemism, *complicated*. One particularly prevalent sin was sexual immorality, apparently including having sex with prostitutes.

The Corinthians had evidently tried to justify this practice with some of the slogans Paul quotes back to them at the start of this passage. "All things are lawful"—in other words, the gospel means I'm now free to do anything. Grace, not law. So it's fine to visit the brothel. "Food is meant for the stomach and the stomach for food"—in other words, the body has appetites that are meant to be satisfied. When we're hungry, that means we're meant to eat; when we're horny, we're meant to have sex. It's just a matter of biology.

Paul counters with his own one-liners: "Not all things are helpful" and "I will not be dominated by anything." Not being under the law doesn't mean we're moral free agents. We're not to be mastered by anything. We're certainly not to pursue what is not beneficial to us. Yes, food is meant for the stomach. But that doesn't mean our sexual desires are meant to be indiscriminately met. More than that, if we're going to talk about something's biological purpose, then we need to recognize that our whole body is meant for the Lord. It has been made for him, not primarily for us. So we mustn't live in any way that contradicts his purpose and design for our bodies. His purposes trump our own fallen cravings and desires.

Comfort

Paul then digs down into the reality of our union with Christ. Twice he says, "Do you not know?" These are things they should have grasped by now. Maybe Paul had himself taught them all this when he had first planted and established the church. Either way, this is not meant to be new doctrine for them. It is foundational.

First, he says, "Do you not know that your bodies are members of Christ?" This is what we have been seeing in the course of this study. We are one with Christ, members of him. Not just in some abstract, theoretical sense but even in our physicality. It is not just our souls that are connected to Jesus—our very bodies are too.

This stuff is real. Your flesh-and-blood body, in whatever health or shape it happens to be in, belongs to Jesus. Our bodies are members of Christ, inseparably part of who he is. This is glorious.

Several years ago, a friend invited me to hike a British mountain with him. I was looking forward to a few hours of good conversation while enjoying the scenery. But my friend was far fitter than I was, and so we spent very little of the route actually hiking together. Mostly, he was way up ahead and would periodically wait for me to catch up before pushing further up ahead.

It can sometimes feel like that with Jesus. Yes, we're his and he's ours, but it can seem as though he's way ahead of us, barely a speck on the horizon. Or maybe we feel as if he's attending to some more important matter at the other end of the universe. But in fact, our union means he is right with us—all the time and forever. There is not a waking moment we ever need to spend away from him. He is closer than anyone else ever could be. As Psalm 23 famously says,

> Even though I walk through the valley of the shadow of
> death,
>   I will fear no evil,
> for you are with me. (Ps. 23:4)

One of the greatest blessings in this life is close, faithful friendship. I've been blessed with more than I deserve—friends who will drop everything in a crisis to come and be with me, who will make sure I don't face any challenges alone. It is wonderful to have friends like that and to try to be a friend like that. But even the very closest human relationships have limitations. There are places where even the most willing friends will not be able to accompany us.

David talks about passing through the valley of the shadow of death. There are dark and fearful places in this world. And death itself is the darkest and most fearful of all. No earthly friend can pass through that with us. In the best circumstances, family and friends might be with us up until our very final breath, but no one can go further than that.

Except Jesus. He is with us, all the way through that valley and out to the green pastures and still waters beyond. He has been through it himself and can take us through it with him. There is no other friend like him.

Motivation

Not only is this truth a deep comfort in times of trouble and fear, but it is also a powerful motivation to pursue holiness. He is with us always. Which means we can't spiritually unhitch ourselves from him to go off and sin and then come back to reattach ourselves. Paul tells us that one of the implications of our bodies being members of Christ is that they remain members of Christ even when we're sinning:

> Do you not know that your bodies are members of Christ? Shall I then take the members of Christ and make them members of a prostitute? Never! (1 Cor. 6:15)

Where we go, we take our union with Christ with us. Our bodies are his, which means all the parts of our bodies are his. The hands with which I'm typing this are his, which means if I go and sin with these hands, I am sinning with *hands that belong to Jesus.* I am taking *his* rightful property and using it to sin.

As mentioned before, some in the church in Corinth were visiting prostitutes. They had taken the "Food is meant for the stomach" principle and really run with it. Sexual appetites need to be met, they reasoned, and the easiest way to satisfy such desires was the convenience of a prostitute. A quick trip to the brothel, and everything would be sorted out. But they either seem not to have known or had grievously forgotten that they take Christ with them when they do so. They can't, as it were, leave him in the car while they go inside. Our union with him is not so casual. We are not loosely tethered to him; we are profoundly one with him. So as these Corinthian readers urgently needed to realize, when you go into a brothel, you are taking Jesus there too.

The upshot of all this? "Flee from sexual immorality" (1 Cor. 6:18). We can hide our sins from one another. We can't hide them from Jesus. We can't choose not to involve him. The word "flee" here is very strong. This isn't like the safety briefings that urge, in the event of a fire, "Calmly make your way to the nearest exit." Paul is meaning something far more intense.

The hardest I have ever yelled at a TV screen was during an episode of the natural history show *Planet Earth II.* One iconic sequence showed a batch of iguanas hatching on a beach and immediately having to run the gauntlet of hungry racer snakes to get to safety.[1] We watch, with mounting tension, as one after another of these iguanas gets its first glimpse of

1   *Planet Earth II*, episode 1, "Islands," directed by Elizabeth White, aired November 6, 2016, on BBC One. (On YouTube this has been viewed many tens of millions of times.)

sunlight and takes its first steps, as the snakes, immediately triggered by the movement, begin racing toward it. In one or two cases, the iguanas are momentarily oblivious to the scaly death bearing down on them like torpedoes. Which is where the shouting starts. "*RUN!!*" What a way to experience your first moments of life.

This is what Paul has in mind. *This* is how urgent it is for us to flee sexual sin. Our union with Jesus gives us every reason to run.

A New Reaction to the Law

But it is not just sexual sin that being in Christ moves us to avoid.

In his letter to the Romans, Paul is at pains to help his readers realize that being in Christ means they are no longer under the Old Testament law of God. He likens it to how a woman is released from the obligations of marriage when her husband dies: "If her husband dies, she is free from that law, and if she marries another man she is not an adulteress" (Rom. 7:3). In marriage, death is the end of the covenant. Widows or widowers should not feel unfaithful if they go on to marry someone else. And Paul wants us to know that this is how it is with the law:

> Likewise, my brothers, you also have died to the law through the body of Christ, so that you may belong to another, to him who has been raised from the dead, in order that we may bear fruit for God. (Rom. 7:4)

Like someone in a marriage, Paul's readers were in a binding arrangement with God's law. But in this instance, it is not the other party that has died and released them from this obligation. Paul says that they *themselves* have died—through Christ and so as to now belong to him and to share in his new life.

Part of what it means to have died in Christ is to have died to the law. Why should this matter? It matters because it is the law that kept triggering sin:

> For while we were living in the flesh, our sinful passions, aroused by the law, were at work in our members to bear fruit for death. (Rom. 7:5)

This is not because of any moral fault in the law itself (as Paul will go on to explain in the verses that follow); it is because of the way our sinful hearts are skewed. Just as a resentful child will often lash out at being given further instructions from a parent, our hearts react against God's demands on us by leaping toward sin. God's ways actually *provoke* us.

I have Crohn's disease, an inflammatory condition in the gut. In one difficult season, things flared up so badly that I couldn't eat or drink anything. But the only medicine I had to treat it with was in the form of pills. Try as I might to take them, my body just couldn't receive anything, and any time I tried to take them, I threw them back up before they could make any difference.

This is how the people of God were with the Old Testament law. They needed all the direction and help God could give through the law, but sinful hearts cannot take in God's ways without, as it were, throwing them up. So the more we keep trying to "take" God's law externally, the more we keep reacting against it and going further into sin.

It is our union with Christ that frees us from this pattern:

But now we are released from the law, having died to that which held us captive, so that we serve in the new way of the Spirit and not in the old way of the written code. (Rom. 7:6)

The only solution to my Crohn's situation was to find a way to take the medicine internally and not externally. It was quickly fixed by a visit to the hospital and a few hours hooked up to a drip.

In our reaction to the law, Jesus does something similar. Our union with him means we have died to the law and been released from its external demands, which our sinful selves could never really accept. It also means that we can now belong to Jesus, be one with him, and live by his Holy Spirit. What couldn't be done externally through the law, Jesus has done internally through his death and resurrection.

Slaying Sin

This new spiritual reality does not mean that our obedience is now automatic. With the medicine I took through the drip, I didn't have to do anything other than lie there, receive it, and let it make its healing difference. With the new life we have in Christ, we *do* need to consciously walk in light of it and continually appropriate it.

Paul puts it most succinctly to the Colossians:

If then you have been raised with Christ, seek the things that are above, where Christ is, seated at the right hand of God. Set your minds on things that are above, not on things that are on earth. For you have died, and your life is hidden with Christ in God. When Christ who is your life appears, then you also will appear with him in glory.

Put to death therefore what is earthly in you: sexual immorality, impurity, passion, evil desire, and covetousness, which is idolatry. (Col. 3:1–5)

Paul makes it clear how we are connected to Christ:

- We have been raised with him.
- We have died with him.
- Our present life is hidden with him.
- We will one day appear with him.

Our union with him is that comprehensive. And because of all that, Paul can say, "Put to death *therefore* what is earthly in you." If "in Christ" is *who* we really are, and if "raised with Christ" is *where* we really are, and if "being like Christ" is where we're really *headed*, then it makes total sense to live in light of that reality now. Our minds should be where our spiritual identity is: with Christ, above, not in what is earthly, below. To continue to cultivate the latter would be to contradict the former. It would be a denial of who we now are in Jesus.

So Paul says to "put to death" all in us that does not belong to our life in Christ. It needs to be that definitive.

Theologians call this *mortification*. If part of the Christian life is what we strain toward, another equally crucial part is what we correspondingly turn away from. I can't pursue holiness if I am not also actively doing away with sin. So as I see "what is earthly" in me, I am to put it to death.

One habit I have tried to develop in light of this teaching is to regularly review my heart to identify which sins most need mortifying. There are often "the usual suspects" that seem especially native to my sinful nature. At times, other sins come to the fore that are not usually big issues for me. But it helps to spend time reflecting before God on what I most need to work on.

Killing sin involves being as aware as we can of two realities: the consequences of sin and the causes of sin. Paul helps us clearly see the consequences:

> But what fruit were you getting at that time from the things of which you are now ashamed? For the end of those things is death. (Rom. 6:21)

Paul mentions two things that follow sin: shame now and death to come. It is not a good benefits package, but we need to remember this. In the moment of temptation, it will feel very different. Sin will seem so warm and good. It will feel like it's on your side and concerned with your happiness. But the reality is vastly different.

There was a story in the UK news a while ago about a house on the coast for sale. It was a cozy little cottage right by the sea, and the picture of it made it look very attractive. But just outside the shot was a nuclear power station, obvious when the cottage was observed from literally any other angle.

Temptation is just like that, offering something that seems initially good but failing to provide the wider picture of what else is involved—a tantalizing attraction dangled right in front of us so that we'll grab it without thinking but not showing us the deep shame that will soon result and the eventual death that all sin will drag us down into unless Christ intervenes. We need to keep this reality at the forefront of our minds.

I became a Christian when I turned eighteen, and I remember in those early days occasionally wondering if it would have been better to have come to faith sometime in my twenties instead, so that I could have had more time to explore sin before repenting. I thought I was missing out. But the exact opposite was in fact the case. God was sparing me not pleasure but deep remorse. Had I experienced a few more years of sin, I wouldn't have pleasant memories to look back on but profound regret and grief. I came to realize that it was a mercy to have been brought to Christ before I had ever had a chance to explore particular sins.

Hebrews puts it with concise realism, talking about how Moses refused "the fleeting pleasures of sin" (Heb. 11:25). We mustn't pretend there is no pleasure to sin; otherwise, we will be naive to the power of temptation. Of course there is pleasure; why else do we fall into sin? But we need to see that it is only *fleeting* pleasure. Whatever pleasure sin brings wears off incredibly fast. Whatever happiness or elation or relief we were looking for is quickly replaced with shame and remorse. Sin never delivers. We think we're getting a quaint cottage by the sea, and we actually end up living next to a revolting power station.

Paul sums it up at the end of his discussion:

For the wages of sin is death, but the free gift of God is eternal life in Christ Jesus our Lord. (Rom. 6:23)

The two alternatives could not be more stark. We face either deserved eternal death apart from Christ or underserved eternal life in him.

As well as being clear on the consequences of sin, we also need to be clear on the causes of it, trying to get to its very root.

I have learned to interrogate the sins that bubble up from within me: *Why* does my heart move toward particular sins in certain moments? It is easy to say, "I was stressed," or "Things were incredibly busy." But that doesn't go far enough. *Why*, when I am feeling stressed, am I impatient with particular individuals? *Why* am I quick to assume that people might be rejecting me? *Why* am I more tempted toward sexual sin if I have just woken up from a dream in which I've let people down?

Sin is often a crude form of self-medication: we are trying to make ourselves feel better or to console ourselves about some particular hurt or deep-seated wound. It helps to know this. It helps us understand the particular soil certain sins tend to spring up in. It helps us then press the gospel further and yet deeper into our hearts.

The first part of the armor of Christ that Paul tells us to put on is the "belt of truth" (Eph. 6:14). The fact is that the devil has done a number on every single one of us. We all inhabit false narratives about who we are, what we're worth, and what God is truly like. Those narratives operate at the macrolevel, such as when we do not come to terms with our fallenness or with the reality that we can be saved only by God's kind grace rather than by our own goodness or religiosity. But they also operate at the granular level too. Moment by moment, in real time, we need to keep seeing the ways in which temptation is lying to us about the goodness of what it is offering or our hearts are lying to us about a sense of worthlessness we feel that seeks relief in some sin or other.

The more purchase we get on the dynamics of our hearts, the more gospel traction we can hope to experience. For me, a sense of letting people down tends to be what often feeds an unhealthy desire for being accepted by others, which can then lead to a path of sexual temptation. Knowing that helps me try to deal with the sin at its very root. First, I try to examine if I actually *have* let everyone down and to realize that I might just be projecting that sense onto circumstances or reading it off some tiny piece of evidence. And second, I remind myself of the deep, pervading acceptance I have in Christ: "If God is for us, who can be against us? . . . Who shall bring any charge against God's elect?" (Rom. 8:31, 33). Even if in my own worst-case scenario I *did* let everyone down, God himself is still *for* me. Even if all others turn their backs on me, *he* never will. My acceptance is through my union with Christ: "There is therefore now no condemnation for those who are in Christ Jesus" (Rom. 8:1). If everyone else was to condemn, the one whose condemnation I should most fear has justified me fully and irreversibly. I can begin to breathe. I'm okay. I'm diminishing the need for my heart to self-medicate through sin. That never works anyway, but the gospel really does.

This is why John can say, in such stark language, "No one who abides in him keeps on sinning" (1 John 3:6). I'm not impervious to temptation, but I am secure in the extraordinary love of God in Christ. Knowing that, more than anything else, is reason to keep living for him.

7

Together in Christ

*We, though many, are one body in Christ, and
individually members one of another.*

ROMANS 12:5

ALTHOUGH I NOW LIVE farther away from my family than I ever
have before, when my birthday rolls around, we still manage to
talk together. My brother is two years older than me and still
maintains that those were the two best years of his life. It was,
he claims, a blissful family of three until I arrived and upended
everything.

But it raises an interesting point. When I was born, I became
a son and a brother at the very same moment.[1] The means of
becoming the one was the very same means of becoming the other.
I couldn't have become a son without also becoming a brother.

---

1   I owe this observation, and the point to which it leads, to Jeremy Treat, *The Atonement: An
    Introduction*, Short Studies in Systematic Theology (Wheaton, IL: Crossway, 2023), 134.

The latter wasn't an option for me. It was a package deal: having Mum and Dad as my parents also meant having their older son as my brother.

Something very similar happens with our union with Christ. Joining him means also being joined to others who are joined to him. We don't get Christ without also getting his people.

The Damascus Principle

Paul learned this lesson dramatically the very moment he first encountered the risen Christ. Up until this point (and then being known primarily as Saul), he had been intent on persecuting the church, overseeing the stoning of Stephen and searching out other Christians so that they could be punished. Luke writes, "Saul was ravaging the church, and entering house after house, he dragged off men and women and committed them to prison" (Acts 8:3). This was not a mild objection to Christianity; it was an almost bestial obsession. Later in life, as an apostle, Paul would write of how he "persecuted the church of God violently and tried to destroy it" (Gal. 1:13). One wonders how hard that sentence would have been to write for someone who was now such a servant of the church. I suspect his hand may have shaken as he penned those words.

So we get the picture of what he had been like. What changed him from trying (in his words) "to destroy" the church to being an apostle and planter of so many churches? Meeting Christ. And the very manner of that encounter takes us to the heart of this chapter.

When Saul met Christ, he was, famously, on the road to the city of Damascus, seeking to flush out and obliterate whatever Christian community could be found there. He was abruptly stopped in his tracks.

Enter Jesus:

> Suddenly a light from heaven shone around him. And falling to
> the ground, he heard a voice saying to him, "Saul, Saul, why are
> you persecuting me?" And he said, "Who are you, Lord?" And
> he said, "I am Jesus, whom you are persecuting." (Acts 9:3–5)

Notice the language being used. Jesus is speaking and says both,
"Why are you persecuting me?" and, "I am Jesus, whom you are
persecuting." We would expect such a voice to say, "Why are
you persecuting *my church*?" and, "I am Jesus, whose *people* you
are persecuting," but in both cases Jesus identifies himself as the
object of Paul's persecution. What Paul is intending to do to them,
he is actually doing to Christ. This is how closely Jesus identifies
with his people. For Jesus, to persecute the church is to persecute
him. Paul's very first moment of exposure to Jesus made this so
devastatingly clear to him.

So it is no surprise that Paul would teach so powerfully on the
connection between our union with Christ and our belonging to
those around us who also are united to him. Through being in
Christ, we come to know God as our Father, which also means
coming to know his people as our brothers and sisters. Being part
of the people of God is not some optional in-app purchase we can
choose to make after we've already become Christians. Being in
Christ means being part of others who are also in him. We don't
get him without them.

And how we treat them (as Paul discovered that day en route
to Damascus) is how we treat him. So this matters. Jesus won't let
us separate our attitude to his people from our attitude to him.

If we are attacking the church, we are attacking Jesus. If we're neglecting the church, we're neglecting Jesus. If we're serving the church, we're serving Jesus. Jesus himself said, "Truly, I say to you, as you did it to one of the least of these my brothers, you did it to me" (Matt. 25:40). The gospel has both vertical and horizontal aspects to it: our union with God above and our concomitant obligation to fellow believers around us. Indeed, as Jeremy Treat notes, the very shape of the cross expresses the inseparability of these two dimensions of our faith:

> The shape of the cross itself is a constant reminder of the comprehensive nature of Christ's work: the vertical beam of the cross is a symbol of the reconciliation between God and sinners, while the horizontal beam is a symbol of God reconciling sinners to one another.[2]

What makes us one with God makes us one with each another.

Wounds in the Church

For many people today, this might feel like a burden being laid on us. Yes, we want to be those who follow Jesus. We trust him. We know he is perfectly faithful and will never let us down. But maybe we can't say the same thing of his people. By definition, every Christian, however transforming Christ's grace has been in his or her life, is still a sinner. In the church we can and do and will let each other down—often in minor, easily forgiven ways but sometimes in very serious ways that can lead to deep and lasting

2 Treat, *Atonement*, 121.

wounds. The church in this world will never be perfect. It would be naive to think that just because people are fellow Christians, they're not going to hurt you; the very fact that someone is a fellow believer can make the hurt even more painful.

In a time (in the West, at least) when we are highly conscious of and sensitive to abuse in society and in the church, we might be tempted to think that we've woken up to something earlier generations knew nothing about and that past expressions of commitment to the local church no longer carry any weight, given what we know and what they didn't. It is true that every generation will have its own set of blind spots and own set of insights. We probably *are* more attuned to some of these things than our immediate forebears. But we mustn't think we're the first generation to realize how challenging churches can be.

The New Testament reflects an unflinching realism about what the people of God can be like. It is not as if the Epistles were written in some idealized time in which the primitive church was problem-free. The very Scriptures that lay out our obligations to our fellow believers are the same Scriptures that also detail some of the ugliest failings of the church.

Take the Corinthian church. Paul's first letter to the Corinthians was one of the more feisty of the letters he wrote. Here we see a church riddled with extraordinary dysfunction.

To be fair, this was a church full of recent believers. Paul had not long before planted this church, so it didn't have older generations of believers to lean on and learn from or much of a history to have been matured by.

But that doesn't minimize the seriousness of these issues. Paul goes so far as to say to them, "In the following instructions I do not commend you, because when you come together it is not for the better but for the worse" (1 Cor. 11:17)—imagine hearing *that* read out at church. This congregational life included the following:

- Open quarrelling over which leaders were more impressive to follow
- Sexual sin of a kind to make pagan onlookers raise an eyebrow (and bear in mind that first-century Corinth was hard to shock)
- A practice of celebrating the Lord's Supper that looked more like a cross between a high school cafeteria, given the apparent pecking order of in-groups and out-groups, and a frat party, given that some went without eating at all while others ended up drunk

And this is just a sampling of some of the things that were going wrong with just one church.

So the New Testament is not naive about what church life can be like. And yet, amazingly, the church in Corinth is still *a church*. Even with that litany of problems ahead of him to deal with, Paul can begin the letter by addressing it,

> To the *church of God* that is in Corinth, to those *sanctified* in Christ Jesus, called to be saints together with all those who in every place call upon the name of our Lord Jesus Christ, both their Lord and ours. (1 Cor. 1:2)

This is highly instructive. This mess of a church whose meetings did more harm than good is still a real, legitimate church. It is a church of God. So Paul is not even just saying it's technically a church because it is part of some recognized denomination. It is a church in *God's* eyes. Moreover, this church is composed of "those sanctified in Christ Jesus." A saint is not a special kind of Christian, someone who has been through some sort of spiritual finishing school. A saint is another word for a Christian. In Christ we are sanctified in the sense of already having been set apart by God to be his people and needing to learn—bit by bit, day by day—how to live out what that actually means.

Paul goes on to say that these Corinthian believers have been "called to be saints together with all those who in every place call upon the name of our Lord." Their own individual status in Christ connects each of them not only to the rest of their own church but even more widely to *all* who name the name of Jesus as they do. There is something unavoidably corporate involved in calling on Christ. He is the common Lord they all share—"both theirs and ours."

The Lord's Prayer and the Corporate Body

Jesus highlights something of this corporate dimension in how he teaches his people to pray. In the larger context, Jesus first underscores how our prayer life is to be unseen rather than put on for show:

> And when you pray, you must not be like the hypocrites. For they love to stand and pray in the synagogues and at the street corners, that they may be seen by others. Truly, I say to you, they have received their reward. But when you pray, go into your room and shut the door and pray to your Father who is in secret. (Matt. 6:5–6)

The kind of prayer Jesus wants us to cultivate here is private and individual, each of us alone before our Father, behind closed doors. He then tells us what to pray:

Pray then like this:

> "Our Father in heaven,
> hallowed be your name . . ." (Matt. 6:9)

The very first word we are to pray in our private, individual prayer is corporate: "*Our* Father." Even praying on our own, we are bringing with us the corporate dimension of our life in Christ.

Back to Corinth. For all its unique flaws, this church was a real church, and its believers therefore had real obligations to one another.

This is not to say that no Christian should ever leave a particular church—at various times I've had to counsel friends to leave churches where it was becoming evident the pastor was ungodly or where the teaching was veering well away from Scripture. But even if such a step is sadly necessary, it doesn't negate the reality that union with Christ still means union with his people. If one particular church is not going to be a healthy place to grow in Christ, we should hope to find one that will.

Joyful Fellowship

No church will be without its messiness. Yet for all the complexities of being part of God's people, the Bible is clear that it is not meant to be seen as merely burdensome.

The apostle John makes the connection between having fellowship with God and fellowship with God's people, and he shows how this encompassing communion ultimately leads to joy:

> That which we have seen and heard we proclaim also to you, so that you too may have fellowship with us; and indeed our fellowship is with the Father and with his Son Jesus Christ. And we are writing these things so that our joy may be complete. (1 John 1:3–4)

As an apostle, John has been an eyewitness of Jesus, physically seeing and hearing him during his earthly ministry. That is a unique privilege we are two millennia too late to enjoy. But we are not missing out. John's proclaiming of all he witnessed gives us an opportunity to come into fellowship with him and his fellow apostles, and—more importantly—into fellowship with the Father and the Son. We see again the gospel bringing both vertical and horizontal fellowship.

And this, John says, is the way to know complete joy. It is likely that the "our" in "our joy" of 1 John 1:4 includes his readers. We all together—apostles, nonapostles, original recipients of the letter, and those of us reading it centuries later—can find deepest joy through these twin realities of fellowship. There is partial joy to be found in many areas of life, even without Christ. But complete, ultimate joy is found only through knowing him and his people. If we think separating ourselves from the fellowship of other believers will make us happier in the long run, we are mistaken. Sometimes the lack of joy we experience in our fellowship with others is because we have not gone far enough in.

Later in the same letter, John reinforces the relationship between our vertical and horizontal fellowships:

> Everyone who believes that Jesus is the Christ has been born of God, and everyone who loves the Father loves whoever has been born of him. By this we know that we love the children of God, when we love God and obey his commandments. (1 John 5:1–2)

Again, the two are inseparable—belonging to Jesus and belonging to his people. John shows us how unthinkable it would be to love the Father and not love those born of him.

Some friends of mine recently had their first child, a beautiful girl. Not long after she was born, I was invited to pop in and meet her. It was, as you would expect, a sweet time. I held her. She didn't cry. We all talked about sleep and feeding rhythms and the usual new-child things. It was special to share in their joy in her.

But just imagine for a moment that as I was leaving I told my friends, "So good to see you, as always. I love you both so much. Let's catch up again soon. But if I'm honest, I *hate* your baby. But I love *you* two. See you soon!"

Irrespective of how much I said I loved them as a couple, a lack of love for their child would obviously reflect a lack of love for *them*. They would be right to question the sincerity and depth of my friendship. As a friend, I can't have them and not their child. They all come together now, as a set. Love for their child is an obvious (and thankfully for me, very natural) expression of my love for them.

The same goes for our relationship with God. If we claim to love him but are cold to those born of him, we have to question whether our love for him is actually real.

An Established Unity

This connection is why the New Testament speaks of our unity with other believers in such important and categorical terms. It is sometimes easy to mistakenly think that the gospel reconciles us to God and reconciles other believers to God, and therefore we have to merely *try* to get along and eke out whatever unity we can. But this is not so. The horizontal union is both as real and as secured by the cross as our vertical union with God. We aren't to try to *create* a unity together as believers; we're to express and live out the unity we *already have*.

Consider these words from Ephesians:

> But now in Christ Jesus you who once were far off have been brought near by the blood of Christ. For he himself is our peace, who has made us both one and has broken down in his flesh the dividing wall of hostility by abolishing the law of commandments expressed in ordinances, that he might create in himself one new man in place of the two, so making peace, and might reconcile us both to God in one body through the cross, thereby killing the hostility. And he came and preached peace to you who were far off and peace to those who were near. (Eph. 2:13–17)

Paul is speaking of two groups: those who "were far off" and those who "were near." It's his way of talking, respectively, about the Gentiles and the Jews. The Gentiles were far off because they were not part of the people of Israel in the Old Testament, living under the covenant Israel had with God. The Jews, in contrast, were near, right where all the spiritual action was. They had the law, the promises, and the temple. Between the two was what Paul describes as "the dividing wall of hostility." These two groups were, in religious terms, oil and water—impossible to mix. This was a division that seemed to transcend ethnic and spiritual difference.

Until Jesus. His death smashed through this wall like a wrecking ball, opening the way for these two groups to come together and form a whole new kind of humanity—a different kind of community than had been seen before.

Notice two things. First, this peace and unity have come about through union with Christ. "In Christ Jesus you . . . have been brought near" (Eph. 2:13). He has created "in himself" a new man (Eph. 2:15). The reconciliation spoken of here cannot be enjoyed outside Christ but only in him. Which means, second, this new unity in Christ has already been established. Paul is speaking in past tense. The wall of hostility has *come down*. It is not still standing, teetering because of what Christ has done but needing us to keep pounding it. The cross does not give us the *potential* to develop unity, as if it provides us with a sort of starter kit from which we can begin to establish the beginnings of some peace between us all. No, the horizontal unity between us is as real and secured as our vertical unity with God. That does not mean we will realize it perfectly in this age, but it does mean that it's real and that we need to live in light of it.

Christ-Based Unity

This reality puts an obligation on us to treat our unity very seriously. Paul's letter to the church in Philippi highlights the significance of this principle:

So if there is any encouragement in Christ, any comfort from love, any participation in the Spirit, any affection and sympathy, complete my joy by being of the same mind, having the same love, being in full accord and of one mind. Do nothing from selfish ambition or conceit, but in humility count others more significant than yourselves. Let each of you look not only to his own interests, but also to the interests of others. (Phil. 2:1–4)

Again we see union with Christ—"encouragement in Christ." And we see its social implication: being of one mind and one love together, living out and embodying the oneness that already exists through Jesus.

This is why division is so serious, as Paul notes:

I entreat Euodia and I entreat Syntyche to agree in the Lord. (Phil. 4:2)

Any disagreement can be difficult. But this kind of disagreement in the church is a contradiction of what we have in Jesus—hence the need for these two women to "agree in the Lord."

In this instance, there doesn't seem to be any serious immorality or doctrinal unfaithfulness—Paul normally calls those things out explicitly. Nor are these two individuals brand-new converts still finding their spiritual feet. Paul says they have "labored side by side with me in the gospel" (Phil. 4:3). We don't know what caused the division between them—whether it was a personality clash, a difference over some secondary theological issue or approach to ministry, or something else. But that Paul thinks it necessary to publicly name each of them shows us how much it concerns him.

They are to "agree in the Lord." The language here is related to that in the earlier passage from Philippians 2. These two women may not end up having all the same opinions, but they are to have the same overall mindset as each other—the same that the whole church is to have and that we find most perfectly expressed in Jesus himself (Phil. 2:5). Our union with Christ demands no less. If we are one together as his people, we need to do all we can to live that out.

Overcoming Divisions

If Paul's urging of Euodia and Syntyche to agree in the Lord shows us the pressing urgency of our unity in Christ, another passage shows us something of its staggering scope. In Galatians our unity transcends our economic status, ethnicity, and biological sex, while not obliterating those distinctions:

> There is neither Jew nor Greek, there is neither slave nor free, there is no male and female, for you are all one in Christ Jesus. (Gal. 3:28)

Paul is not saying that there is now no such thing as being Jewish or Greek, slave or free, male or female, as if all those distinctions no longer exist. A free Greek woman who comes to faith remains free, Greek, and a woman. Her present economic status, ethnicity, and biological sex are not erased by her becoming a Christian. Paul's point is that in our justification, those distinctions make no difference. We all come to Christ in exactly the same way, whatever our background or place in this world. It is not like the security area at the airport, with one line for those who have some particular status that expedites the process and another for everyone else. We all come to Christ the same way. There is only one lane—faith in Christ and what he has done on the cross. Being slave or free, Jew or Greek, a man or a woman makes no difference. All alike have fallen short of God's glory; all alike rely solely on the free grace of God to us in Christ. In this we are "all one in Christ Jesus"—brought together through him, united at the foot of the cross. This is revolutionary.

It is part of fallen human nature to divide. We're all different. We can't help but notice it. And having noticed it, we start to evaluate each other on the basis of it, which in turn leads to value judgments, discrimination, resentment, and conflict. Every society lives with its own particular legacy of this dividing. In some it will be more obviously gender based, with women being less "free" (to use Paul's language) than men. In others it might be particular groups that are favored over others. We think of apartheid in South Africa, the caste system in India, Malaysia's policy of privileging ethnic Malays over other groups, or the enslaving of Africans and subsequent withholding of key civil rights from them in America. Division and injustice are the norm for human nature. Education and legislation can make some significant differences. But Paul is showing us something more deeply radical.

In Galatians we see how groups that might otherwise have been at loggerheads can now truly be "one"—by being one in Christ Jesus. Unity through Christ is more foundationally transformative than anything else in this world. There is simply no earthly human difference, of any kind, that the gospel of Jesus cannot overcome. Once the "dividing wall of hostility" between Jew and

Gentile came tumbling down, it was inevitable that all other such divisions would start collapsing as soon as the gospel came along.

Jesus, the Cross, and Unity

No wonder we therefore see Jesus, just hours before his death, praying for the unity of his people:

> I do not ask for these only, but also for those who will believe in me through their word, that they may all be one, just as you, Father, are in me, and I in you, that they also may be in us, so that the world may believe that you have sent me. The glory that you have given me I have given to them, that they may be one even as we are one, I in them and you in me, that they may become perfectly one, so that the world may know that you sent me and loved them even as you loved me. (John 17:20–23)

Jesus is praying for what will be accomplished through his imminent suffering. These requests here are not pie-in-the-sky, make-a-wish aspirations. Jesus is staring at the nearing cross, what he must do there, and all that will flow from it. The outcome of this request is not hanging in the balance; it is part of what his finished work was always intended to bring about. This prayer is recorded for us not so that we can try to create the unity Jesus dreamed of in his final moments but so that we can understand and live in light of the unity he has already secured.

Notice who the prayer is concerned with. He has been praying for the apostles with him at the Last Supper. Now he prays for all who "will believe" in him—every future generation of believers. This prayer encompasses you and me if we are Christians.

Jesus is not being vague in how he defines those believers. They are those who (1) "believe in me" and (2) believe "through their [i.e., the apostles'] word." Both aspects are vital. Jesus himself must be the object of faith. There is no possibility of spiritual unity with someone who, say, believes in "God" but remains unconvinced by Jesus. There is no other name under heaven by which we can be saved (Acts 4:12). Belief in Jesus is nonnegotiable.

But also, the Jesus being believed in must be the one presented through the teaching of the apostles. Jesus commissioned his apostles to bring his word to the world to establish the church. We have that word recorded for us in the New Testament. Jesus expects *that* apostolic word to bring people to faith in him. There is no possibility of spiritual unity with someone who believes in a Jesus who in any way contradicts the apostles' teaching. True Christian unity is not the unity of everyone who simply claims to be a Christian, irrespective of what that claim might consist of; it is an actual unity of all who have come to exclusive faith in the real Jesus of the New Testament.

Jesus prays that these future believers would not just be one but be one in a particular kind of way. Twice he grounds this oneness in the oneness he himself enjoys with the Father:

Just as you, Father, are in me, and I in you, that they also may be in us. (John 17:21)

. . . even as we are one, I in them and you in me, that they may become perfectly one. (John 17:22–23)

The unity Jesus has with the Father is the unity that we have with the Father and the Son and that we also have with one another as his people. The oneness of the Trinity has been opened up so that we can be enfolded into it, enjoying and embodying it ourselves.

This is not a unity we can hope to concoct ourselves. There are all kinds of "oneness" in the world today. We see a form of oneness when a community pulls together for some common cause or when friends rally around someone in great need. In the wake of national tragedies or threats, we see something of the same thing. It can be wonderful. Strangers talk to each other. People start to give each other the benefit of the doubt. Everyone seems to come together. But as time goes by and normal life moves on, the old cracks begin to resurface, and the divisions we had momentarily set aside reappear.

But the oneness Jesus is talking about is of a very different species. Its origin is in heaven itself. It is of a different kind of order.

Everyday Unity

Someone once told me that "life is a sum of trivialities." It tends to be the small things that, accumulated, are most consequential, rather than the big headline moments. Real life tends to happen in the everyday granular moments.

I was thinking of this idea while looking through some of my friend Leslie's photo albums. For years now she has maintained the discipline of trying to take at least one photo every day and then compiling them all into a physical, printed album at the end of each year. She has quite the collection by now. Thumbing through a couple of them, I was struck by how many of my own photos tend to be of the special events—big trips, vacations, birthdays, Christmases—and how much I appreciated Leslie having a record of the everyday and regular—coffee with a neighbor, what the garden looked like on a random November morning, a typical weekday dinner, card games on the weekend, a Sunday afternoon walk. Unexceptional on their own but profoundly exceptional in aggregate. Life is like that. The norms count for more than the exceptions.

So it is not surprising to see that the unique togetherness Christ brings about operates at that kind of level. The New Testament presents us with a sweeping range of "one another" commands that might strike us as perhaps a little mundane:

Be kind to one another. (Eph. 4:32)

Serve one another. (Gal. 5:13)

Welcome one another. (Rom. 15:7)

Live in . . . harmony with one another. (Rom. 15:5)

[Bear] with one another. (Eph. 4:2)

These do not feel dramatic. Hollywood movies tend not to reach their climax with things like *kindness* and *bearing*. We might expect coming-kingdom activity to be more high-octane.

But all the New Testament "one anothers," put together in aggregate, could not better outline the kind of heavenly unity that has descended to Christ's people here on earth. Behind each seemingly innocuous command lies a whole new way of thinking and being. Take just one example, one of the most repeated— to encourage one another:

Let us consider how to stir up one another to love and good works, not neglecting to meet together, as is the habit of some, but *encouraging one another*, and all the more as you see the Day drawing near. (Heb. 10:24–25)

As I write this, it is exactly eighty days until Christmas. That doesn't mean endless, frantic preparation just yet. But it is a reminder that I already need to start doing some things—at this stage, booking flights to be home with the family. And as we get closer, I'll need to think of gifts for people, put together some Advent sermons, and hang decorations. (I'm worried the eighty-day mark is going to trigger my housemate to start playing Christmas music.)

The writer to the Hebrews is making a similar point. Another day is on the horizon, far more consequential, and—in this case— we don't know how many days away it is, other than being one day less far away than it was yesterday. As that day draws ever nearer, it focuses us on how we need to live. Jesus will be returning soon. We will be perfectly united with him in all fullness and glory. And one of the ways we prepare for that perfected oneness with him is by investing heavily in our relationships with one another.

By the time this letter was being written, some had already stopped meeting together as God's people. "Christianity without church" is not a new idea. Hence the writer re-ups the call to meet together.

But notice how the point is being made: "not neglecting to meet . . . but encouraging one another." The opposite of not meeting together isn't meeting together but *encouraging* one another. That one word seems to encapsulate the net effect of all the other "one another" activities that take place when we gather. Our overall goal with each other as fellow believers is to encourage each other. God has designed us to need this—to need the encouragement of others and for them to need the encouragement of each of us.

So as we think about our lives together in Christ, we need to have at least two points of focus. First is the encouragement we need from others. Regularly skipping church and other forms of being together ultimately deprives ourselves of something God considers vital to us. We are not so spiritually self-contained that we don't need the input, counsel, bearing, ministry, love, and *encouragement* of other Christian men and women. So each Sunday as I make my way to church, there are worse ways of preparing than to pray that I would be encouraged, which means praying that I would be consciously *willing to receive* encouragement.

But second, it also means I need to pray that I would be an encouragement. For some of us, the problem might be thinking that we're really not needed, that we have nothing to offer, that our presence makes no real difference to anyone else—that no one will be the poorer if we're not there.

But this is not so. It can't be. You are no less "in Christ" than anyone. You have as much of Jesus in you as they do. You *cannot* be insignificant. You have a God-given capacity (or he wouldn't have commanded this) to be a real encouragement to other Christians. You might not necessarily know exactly *how* you are so, but you can be sure *that* you are so. So this is also something to pray about: that you would long to find ways to encourage and bless those fellow believers God has put around you.

The more we anticipate further union with Jesus, the more we lean into our togetherness in him. Straining toward him means straining toward him together.

Continuing in Christ

*Therefore, as you received Christ Jesus
the Lord, so walk in him.*

COLOSSIANS 2:6

MOST COUNTRIES HAVE a national symbol drawn from the natural world. My home country, England, has the lion as a national emblem, which has always struck me as a little fanciful, given their distinctive lack of natural abundance. Scotland, more realistically, opted for the thistle; Wales, less realistically, the red dragon. The United States, my adopted home, went for the eagle, which is both imposing *and* naturally occurring. Our Canadian friends opted for only the latter of these in going for the maple leaf.

One of the principal national symbols of Israel in biblical times was the vine. It was an apt symbol, given Israel's story. The vine spoke of who they were and what they were about. They had been planted in the land by God himself. He had tended and cared for them. They did not exist for their own sake primarily but to bear fruit for him. In their national character, they were to demonstrate something of what it meant to be his people. They were to reflect who he was and what he was like.

And yet for much of their history, their performance was mixed at best. They had not been the people they were meant to be. As a vine, they had become wild and unkempt, producing either no fruit or bad fruit. This diagnosis had been given to them by God himself at various points:

> For the vineyard of the Lord of hosts
> > is the house of Israel,
> and the men of Judah
> > are his pleasant planting;
> and he looked for justice,
> > but behold, bloodshed;
> for righteousness,
> > but behold, an outcry! (Isa. 5:7)

> Restore us, O God of hosts;
> > let your face shine, that we may be saved!

> You brought a vine out of Egypt;
> > you drove out the nations and planted it. . . .

> Turn again, O God of hosts!
> > Look down from heaven, and see;
> have regard for this vine,
> > the stock that your right hand planted. (Ps. 80:7–8, 14–15)

In both passages, Israel is the vineyard and is not producing what it was meant to—and indeed, is producing what is unwanted: injustice and wickedness. The prevailing need is restoration. The vineyard is not fit for its purpose.

So Jesus's own use of the vineyard language is not innocuous. Over the course of the Gospel of John, Jesus has been making a succession of "I am" statements: "I am the good shepherd" (John 10:11); "I am the way, and the truth, and the life" (John 14:6); "I am the bread of life" (John 6:35); and so on. All these are huge claims. All of them reflect something of the uniqueness of who he was and why he came. None of them can we claim to be for ourselves. But perhaps none was as directly challenging to his original hearers as this: "I am the true vine" (John 15:1).

It is not hard to see what Jesus is doing. He is making a claim not just about himself but about the people of Israel at that time. He is the *true* vine, what the people of God were always meant to be, whereas they are not. He embodies and reflects all of what it means to know God. Claiming to be the true vine is a huge statement about himself and a devastating critique of them.

This is something Jesus has demonstrated throughout his earthly ministry. He has been showing us ways in which he embodies all that God's people were meant to be and yet failed to be. D. A. Carson points out how the temptations of Jesus, for example, "repeated in a personal way the kind of testing Israel faced as God's 'son' during the 40 years in the wilderness (see Deut. 6–8). That national 'son' failed the tests repeatedly but Jesus here triumphed in His."[1] So Jesus's claim to be the true vine is

---

1 D. A. Carson, *God with Us: Themes from Matthew* (Ventura, CA: Regal Books, 1985), 26.

not a bolt out of the blue. It has been apparent throughout his whole earthly life. Jesus himself is uniquely the people of God. The ultimate, true Israel is this one man.

This is why we can become part of the true people of God only by being united to him. And having become united to him, we need to remain in him. Jesus's language about him being the vine and us the branches makes this point. Notice Jesus's emphasis on the need to abide in him:

> *Abide* in me, and I in you. As the branch cannot bear fruit by itself, unless it *abides* in the vine, neither can you, unless you *abide* in me. I am the vine; you are the branches. Whoever *abides* in me and I in him, he it is that bears much fruit, for apart from me you can do nothing. If anyone does not *abide* in me he is thrown away like a branch and withers; and the branches are gathered, thrown into the fire, and burned. If you *abide* in me, and my words *abide* in you, ask whatever you wish, and it will be done for you. By this my Father is glorified, that you bear much fruit and so prove to be my disciples. As the Father has loved me, so have I loved you. *Abide* in my love. (John 15:4–9)

Branches that don't remain part of the tree quickly wither and die. Branches that remain stay alive. The key is to stay connected, to abide.

We see the same principle all around us. It's summertime in my adopted home of Nashville, and early this morning it happens to be unusually cool—enough so for me to be able to sit and work outside for a couple of hours before the day really heats up. So I'm wondering which will force me back indoors first: the temperature creeping up or my laptop battery dying. Both are guaranteed: it is the nature of Tennessean summer days to quickly get uncomfortably hot and humid and the nature of this computer to run out of juice.

Laptops do this. However much they are able to do, however high-end they might be, however powerful they are, the moment you unplug them, it is inevitable that they'll eventually lose power.

Our relationship with Jesus is similar. The moment we disconnect from him, we lose spiritual power. We need to remain in Jesus in order to be spiritually healthy. Paul makes a similar point:

> Therefore, as you received Christ Jesus the Lord, so walk in him, rooted and built up in him and established in the faith, just as you were taught, abounding in thanksgiving. (Col. 2:6–7)

Being *in* him means never needing to go *beyond* him. So what is involved in abiding in the true vine? Jesus mentions four things.

Being Pruned

Jesus is the vine. We are the branches. But there is a third element to the analogy that Jesus wants us to understand:

> I am the true vine, and my Father is the vinedresser. Every branch in me that does not bear fruit he takes away, and every branch that does bear fruit he prunes, that it may bear more fruit. (John 15:1–2)

God the Father is the gardener. And we see him doing two things: taking away the branches that don't bear fruit and pruning the ones that do. Notice that no branch escapes the blade. None are left alone. There is no third category of branch that just keeps quiet. Every branch gets cut: either cut back or cut off. The latter are discarded:

> If anyone does not abide in me he is thrown away like a branch and withers; and the branches are gathered, thrown into the fire, and burned. (John 15:6)

We have had something of an example of this principle just a short while earlier in John's Gospel. Judas had been one of the apostles all along. Outwardly, he had looked as much part of all that was going on as his fellow apostles. He had every appearance of being a key member of Team Jesus. He was part of the unique band of those Jesus first called to be his apostles. He shared the same food, even the very same bread and cup as Jesus. When Jesus first indicated that he knew of Judas's betrayal, telling him, "What you are going to do, do quickly," no one else present had any idea what was going on. Judas had evidently showed no obvious sign of his plot against Jesus. So when he finally left to execute his plan, John underscores it for us: "So, after receiving the morsel of bread, he immediately went out. And it was night" (John 13:30).

Judas had looked connected to Jesus. But his leaving showed that he ultimately wasn't. That "it was night" outside only added to the dark sense of foreboding about what was happening to him on the inside. He did not remain and, as with fruitless branches on a vine, was "taken away."

But the branches that remain are pruned. Continuing with Christ will not be easy.

A church I previously attended had some land that was used as a garden. A couple of times a year, we would have a "garden work party" (three words that really don't belong together!). The aim was to tidy up the garden, either tucking it in for the winter months or getting it shipshape and ready for the spring and summer. Overseeing all this was our resident gardening expert, Maureen.

Maureen quickly detected that I had little to no gardening skills. My track record with even robust houseplants tends to be that they swiftly die. So given that my skills lean more toward the destructive rather than the constructive side, Maureen figured she might as well put this to use and gave me the job of pruning some of the trees.

I dutifully obliged, diligently cutting away the branches as small piles of tree debris started to build. After a while, Maureen came over to see my progress. I stood back with an air of pride at my work, the tree in question looking smartly trimmed. But Maureen was unimpressed: I had not cut anywhere near deep enough. She showed me how to do it, and I was immediately appalled at how much she cut back. I had only been nibbling away at the edges, performing the arboreal equivalent of a "short back and sides." She was going for the full head shave. So following her example, I started cutting back much further.

This time, there weren't little mounds of branch ends on the ground. There was a *huge* amount of verdant-looking foliage piling up around me. More was coming off the tree than was remaining on it. It might have looked like I *hated* it.

I realized that day that pruning looks cruel and wasteful. By the time it was done, the branches looked like stumps. But that's pruning. Doing this work enables the branches to grow back with even more life and fruit.

So we need to come to terms with this aspect of our ongoing life in Christ. It will not be painless. There will be pruning for us. The divine cutters might feel very sharp and severe. It might look as though God is being cruel, cutting things that seem healthy and good. Parts of our life are suddenly cut from us and falling to the ground—things that brought us joy and that are painful to lose. Precious relationships perhaps. Or our health or means. Maybe what seemed like a wonderful ministry opportunity.

But this is what Jesus always said it would be like:

> If anyone would come after me, let him deny himself and take up his cross and follow me. For whoever would save his life will lose it, but whoever loses his life for my sake and the gospel's will save it. (Mark 8:34–35)

Proper pruning often looks like it is killing the plant. There may well be times when it feels as though Jesus is actually killing us.

Being cut is never pleasant. The most physical pain I have ever experienced was after an abdominal surgery in which the post-op pain relief did not work. I had been assured by the pain-relief specialist that I would wake up from surgery and "not feel a thing." But the epidural they had administered hadn't numbed the correct part of my anatomy, leaving the wound largely unaffected. (The next two epidurals misfired too.) So it was a very rough experience. But none of that pain took away from the larger reality of what had happened: the surgery had been urgently needed and was for the sake of significantly improving my health. The surgeon's blade had ultimately been healing and not harmful, even though it had led to a lot of pain.

So it is with God. There will be times of pruning for us that may hurt profoundly. Scripture repeatedly tells us that spiritual growth comes through suffering:

> We rejoice in our sufferings, knowing that suffering produces endurance, and endurance produces character, and character produces hope, and hope does not put us to shame. (Rom. 5:3–5)

> Count it all joy, my brothers, when you meet trials of various kinds, for you know that the testing of your faith produces steadfastness. And let steadfastness have its full effect, that you may be perfect and complete, lacking in nothing. (James 1:2–4)

Whatever pain pruning may bring, the one wielding the blade is unfathomably good. This is a gardener we can always fully trust. He will do what is for our long-term good. Which takes us to what Jesus says next. Suffering leads to character, trials to steadfastness, pruning to *fruitfulness*.

Being Fruitful

I once shared an apartment with a friend who had a beloved bonsai tree. He gave this tree all the careful attention it needed, fussing over it, constantly clipping and feeding it. You might already sense that this story is not going to have a happy ending.

One day I was cleaning the kitchen and, having wiped down the sink, decided to leave some bleach in it to soak and get rid of some of the more stubborn grime. Just as I was finishing up, my friend walked in, bonsai in hand, and, thinking the clear liquid in the sink was water, dipped the base of the tree in to give it a drink. The beloved bonsai soon turned yellow and departed this world. Like I said, I am incompetent with plants. But it is not intentional! I feel like Angela Lansbury in *Murder, She Wrote*: not having murderous intent myself but just finding that everything around me ends up dying.

But God is not like me—or any of us—in this regard. When it comes to the vineyard, this vinedresser is an expert. He knows exactly what he is doing. He is the master gardener. His purpose is to make fruitful branches even more so:

> Every branch that does bear fruit he prunes, that it may bear more fruit. (John 15:2)

The fruit of a vine is the grape. The fruit of a Christian is something far more desirable—becoming more and more like Jesus: "The fruit of the Spirit is love, joy, peace, patience, kindness, goodness, faithfulness, gentleness, self-control" (Gal. 5:22–23). Jesus likewise mentions love and joy in John 15:

> This is my commandment, that you love one another as I have loved you. (John 15:12)

> These things I have spoken to you, that my joy may be in you, and that your joy may be full. (John 15:11)

He has already given his disciples his unique peace:

Peace I leave with you; my peace I give to you. Not as the world gives do I give to you. (John 14:27)

For those who know and love Jesus, the thought of bearing this fruit is mouthwatering. We long to be more like him. We long to better reflect who he is to the world around us. We long to be a means by which others come to see him as we do.

Such fruit can come only through Jesus: "Apart from me you can do nothing" (John 15:5). So too with literal branches. Branches do not produce fruit; they bear it. Without the vine it is attached to, branches will bear nothing. No grapes ever appeared on a dead branch.

But with Jesus there is not only the *possibility* of fruit but the *promise* of it—and not just of *some* fruit but of *much* fruit:

Whoever abides in me and I in him, he it is that bears much fruit. (John 15:5)

It is, wonderfully, an inevitability. God wants us to be fruitful and prunes us to that end, and Christ enables us to be fruitful, sharing his life in us and bringing transformation to us. This is so important for us to grasp. We can easily feel defeated in our Christian lives. We can easily think that we will never change, that we are doomed to live in the same failings time and time again. But that is to limit Jesus. How can we come into such an intimate union with him and not be changed? We will not yet become all that we are meant to be—for that we await the new creation. But there is no way we will remain stuck in what we used to be. Fruit will come.

In the movie *Titanic*, after the ship has struck the iceberg, there are still those who think it will be possible to save it. But the shipbuilder who designed the Titanic, Thomas Andrews, knows better. To the man who insists it will not sink, he replies, "She is made of iron, sir. I assure you, she can. And she *will*. It is a mathematical certainty."[2] The flooding of the vessel, her heavy composition, and the unyielding reality of gravity all make it inevitable.

In a reverse of this reality, the invincible buoyancy of Christ in our sunken lives means that it is impossible for us not to rise up. We will bear fruit. It is also a mathematical certainty. And for those who already do, there is the promise of bearing even more fruit. Whoever we are, and at whatever stage of Christian maturity, there is always yet *more* fruit to be borne. We've never reached the maximum possible. All of us have room to grow, and all of us *will* grow!

Being Obedient

Remaining in Jesus involves his words remaining in us:

> If you abide in me, and my words abide in you, ask whatever you wish, and it will be done for you. (John 15:7)

This word has already come to us if we are followers of Jesus:

> Already you are clean because of the word that I have spoken to you. (John 15:3)

---

2   *Titanic*, directed by James Cameron (Los Angeles, CA: Paramount Pictures, 1997), DVD, 195 min.

Jesus's word has already come to us with cleansing power. It is a word that now needs to remain.

I was recently staying at a bed-and-breakfast on a brief break with some friends. The moment we checked in, the proprietors made it very clear that this was a *bed-and-breakfast* and not a *hotel*. The main difference had to do with timings. Breakfast itself was served only within a fairly narrow time frame, and our rooms were not "ours" for the duration of the day but needed to be vacated during office hours and so were available only in the evening and until breakfast. We needed to be out as much as we were in.

So we were staying at this establishment, but we were not *living* there. It really was just meant to be a bed for the night, a quick bite in the morning (only between 7:30 and 8:15 a.m., mind you), and nothing more. Clearly, they *needed* guests for their business but didn't seem to really *want* them. We were tolerated more than we were welcomed.

It is easy for us to be like this with the words of Jesus. We (might) let them into our lives at limited times, perhaps just for a few minutes in the morning. But once we've closed our Bible, those words are effectively meant to be out for the rest of the day so that we can get on unencumbered by them.

But Jesus is calling us to more than this. His words are to *abide* in us. We are to be a permanent dwelling place for them that these words "so lodge in the disciple's mind and heart that conformity to Christ, obedience to Christ, is the most natural (supernatural?) thing in the world."[3]

3   D. A. Carson, *The Gospel according to John*, Pillar New Testament Commentary (Leicester, UK: Apollos, 1991), 517.

This will not happen if we are not striving to *know* Jesus's words. When we use our phones as alarms in the morning, it is all too easy (I did this myself today) to grab the phone and then immediately start looking at whatever notifications have come overnight. Before we know it, we're reading emails, responding to messages, looking at links we've been sent, catching the day's news through social media, and before we are even out of bed, our heads are so swimming in lots of other people's agendas that we never really get to the words of Jesus. Better to set things up such that his words might be the first we receive at the start of the day so that the rest of the day is shaped by what *he* has said.

But receiving the words of Jesus means more than just hearing them: "Be doers of the word, and not hearers only, deceiving yourselves" (James 1:22). Christ's words are meant to have agency in our lives, reordering and reshaping them. We're not just to revere them but to follow them, obeying all that Christ calls us to do.

Remaining in Jesus is bound up with obeying him:

As the Father has loved me, so have I loved you. Abide in my love. If you keep my commandments, you will abide in my love, just as I have kept my Father's commandments and abide in his love. (John 15:9–10)

At first glance, it might seem as if Jesus is saying that obedience is what makes him love us. Yet that would not only completely contradict the heart of the gospel but would also mean that none of us ever received his love. We could never be obedient enough. No, obeying his commands is not how we *earn* his love but how we *remain in* his love. He gives his love to us freely and lavishly through his death and resurrection. And once we receive that love, we are to stay put and remain in it—to bask in it. And obedience is key.

This is not a cold, dry obedience, in which we are formally committed to his ways but resentful of them in our hearts. As we obey what he has commanded, we have ongoing exposure to his love for us. Every single thing our King calls us to do expresses his goodness and care. King David experienced this sense himself: "The commands of the LORD are radiant" (Ps. 19:8 NIV). His commands are radiant because *he* is radiant.

This awareness isn't always immediate. Many of God's commandments initially land on us as all cost and seemingly little benefit. We might find them confounding, going right against so many of our deepest desires. But over time, we come to realize that what feels like a cost is really a gain. What we lose is what was only going to hinder us in our walk with God. There's far more satisfaction on offer through obedience than disobedience. His commands, maybe somewhat unwelcome and frustrating at first, become a felt blessing. It's not always easy, but his words are always radiant.

As we walk with the Lord, we see more and more the goodness of his ways. Maybe some commands will always be a particular struggle. But to resent his law or to want to change it is to say that we know better than God. To follow his ways, even if initially through gritted teeth, declares that we're trusting that God knows more than we do. The more we obey, the more aware we become of the love in which we abide. So rather than thinking we will obey only certain commands *when* we like them, we should instead resolve to obey them *so that* we like them.

Being Prayerful

Jesus weaves prayer into this whole section:

> If you abide in me, and my words abide in you, ask whatever you wish, and it will be done for you. (John 15:7)

> You did not choose me, but I chose you and appointed you that you should go and bear fruit and that your fruit should abide, so that whatever you ask the Father in my name, he may give it to you. (John 15:16)

We begin to realize how intertwined these different aspects of remaining in Jesus really are—obedience, fruitfulness, prayer, all playing off one another. They are distinguishable but not separable. The Christian life is not like a buffet, in which you simply choose what to take and what to leave. It is more like an ecosystem, in which all the different elements depend on one another to be present and flourishing. So we cannot expect to see our prayer lives deepening if we are not also living in obedience; we cannot expect to see much progress in our fruitfulness if we are not making time to cherish the words of Jesus.

Jesus makes a couple of assumptions about prayer.

First, he expects it to be regular. The implication of these verses is that prayer is an ongoing feature of our life with him.

Sometimes we need to be in constant communication with another person. I recently helped a friend from out of town navigate his way to my house for the first time. He shared his location with me and had me on speakerphone directing him. Another time, a friend in another state was walking home late one night and feeling somewhat anxious, so I stayed on the phone with him until he was back safe and sound.

The Christian life is also one of those times. We need to be in ongoing prayer contact with our heavenly Father. Paul tells us to "[pray] at all times" (Eph. 6:18) and to "pray without ceasing" (1 Thess. 5:17) for this reason.

There is never a bad time to pray. It doesn't matter what we're doing, who we're with, or how we feel. It is always a good time to pray. God is *that* available to us, that ready to hear us and help us. We tend to make a parallel with human parents and how a dad, say, will love to help a child who comes to him in need. But the fact is that there is always some limit with human parents. We don't have limitless capacity and unending emotional resources. But God does. We can *always* come to him. And as we seek to remain in Christ, endure pruning, bear fruit, and live in obedience, we will always be needing to come before God in prayer. Growth in the Christian life is needing God more, not needing him less. So we will be doing more asking over the years, not less asking. We don't grow out of prayer, just further into it.

Second, Jesus anticipates our prayer to be effective. Both times he mentions an expectation that what we ask will be done for us, that what we request will be given. He uses very expansive terms: "whatever you wish" and "whatever you ask."

We are not dramatically limited in what we ask for. Yes, we should not ask for what would be evil or selfish, but it is sometimes tempting to think that that must mean only a small band of possibility is left open for us. But in fact, the range of what we can pray for is wide open—joyful prayers and sorrowful prayers, short prayers and long prayers, prayers when we know what we're trying to say and prayers when we don't, big prayers and modest prayers. God can move the nations and also number our hairs, so we mustn't think he's too grand to attend to the details of our lives or too measly to deal with the big things. We can pray for anything.

If we are to be expansive in what we ask for, Jesus shows us to expect God to be expansive in how he responds. We are to pray with confident expectation, not shrinking defeat. Part of the reason for this confidence is not that we've "nailed" prayer—who of us honestly thinks that is the case? Rather, it is that as we remain in Jesus in ever-growing fruitfulness and obedience, our hearts will have been incrementally, maybe to us imperceptibly, changing to be more and more like his, so that what we instinctively find ourselves asking for is more and more aligned with his purposes. Prayer is not about bending God to our wills but about expressing our own wills as they are being bent to his.

That God is so poised to give to us, so trigger-happy with his good gifts, is all because of who we are in Jesus. It is why prayer is in his name. If I were to come to God on the basis of my own performance, I would have no reason to expect to be heard, let alone answered. But coming in the name of Jesus means coming wrapped in his perfect sonship.

Many years ago I booked a flight with an airline that someone I know happens to fly for. After I made the booking, I let him know, and he told me he would see if he could be scheduled as the pilot on that particular route. Nearer the time, he confirmed that he was and told me to meet him at the departure gate. Once there, he told me that I should make myself known to the cabin crew when I boarded and tell them I was "a friend of the captain." Even before I opened my mouth, one of the crew said, "You're with the captain, aren't you?" and whisked me to the cockpit to say hi. From that point on, I was treated to the best flight I've ever had in my life: full use of the first-class cabin, menu, and amenities; trips to the cockpit to chat with the captain and take in the views; a cabin crew that couldn't do enough for me, even presenting me with a goody bag at the end of the flight and thanking *me* for being their special guest. Needless to say, it made all subsequent flights somewhat disappointing by comparison.

All this happened because I was with the captain. Had I come onto that flight in just my own name, I would have been sat way at the back in seat 68E and given no special treatment. But I was stepping onto the plane in *his* name and as *his* friend. As such, I came in at his level, and so all the courtesies and privileges that would have been rightfully his were extended to me.

It is like this in our relationship with Jesus. When we come to the Father in the name of the Son, we come in at the Son's level. In the Gospels, we hear Jesus addressing the Father as "Abba" (Mark 14:36), and we now get to address him in the same intimate way (Rom. 8:15; Gal. 4:6). It is not presumption on our part; it is union with the perfect Son. We don't need to worry about breaking the ice with God or establishing a rapport. He is already more eager to hear our prayers than we are to offer them. The call to abide is as much an invitation as it is a command.

Communion with Christ

What Jesus is urging on us reflects the difference between *union* with Christ and *communion* with him. Union is our relationship with him as those now in him; communion is our working out and enjoyment of that union as we continue to walk with him. It is important to understand this distinction. Our union with Christ is unchanging, whereas our walk with him will inevitably fluctuate as we grow in our relationship with him. There will be times when I am more attentive to my relationship with Jesus and other times when I might neglect it.

We can get this wrong in two ways. We can think that our union is determined by our communion, such that it is our communing with Christ that establishes our union with him. This would put an intolerable burden on our own discipline and rob us of any real assurance.

An analogy might help. I am using a language-learning app to pick up some Spanish, and there are lots of incentives and reminders about maintaining a daily streak. The more days in a row I do it, the more bonuses and rewards the app gives me. It's as if missing a day will automatically undo all the progress I've made. It is easy to think of the Christian life in similar terms, needing to maintain a 365-day streak each year lest our union with Jesus might unravel before our very eyes.

But this is not how our relationship with Jesus works. Even when I am neglecting my communion with Christ, my union with him is secure. I am not less "in him" on a given day just because I might have failed to read my Bible or pray. Similarly, if I fail to call my parents for a long time, that doesn't mean I'm not their son.

But it might make me a *poor* son, which leads to the second way we can get this wrong. If it's unhealthy to think that our communion is what our union depends on, it is also unhealthy to think that the security of our union means our communion doesn't matter.

So we need to abide—to welcome the pruning, to rejoice in the fruitfulness that results, to obey all that our good Lord commands, all the while enjoying expectant access to him in prayer. Such is the Christian life. Such is the privilege of those in Christ.

Conclusion

SHORTLY AFTER I FINALLY acknowledged my middle age and started wearing glasses, I found myself at an event sitting next to a dear friend of mine. As friends tend to do, he started ribbing me about my need for glasses and decided to try them on, "just to see how blind you really are," as he put it.

He immediately gasped. He had expected to see murky, blurred images. Instead, he saw everything with crystal clarity.

Like me, he didn't realize he needed them. He knew *I* did, enough to gently tease me about it. He has worn glasses ever since.

I hope you might have gone through something of a similar experience over the course of this book. Maybe this talk of being "in Christ" felt like a bit of an eccentricity, something others might choose to be into but not really relevant to your own life. If so, I hope that's no longer the case. In any event, if you're still somewhat nonplussed by the whole thing, rest assured that either I've done a poor job explaining it or you've done a poor job understanding it. My money is on the first, for what it's worth. In which case, please keep looking at this topic.

My first venture into thinking about all this was well over a decade ago now. But it has been the single biggest blessing to me since my own conversion. Someone once interviewed me for a ministry team and asked which doctrine, in particular, had most helped me in my personal Christian life. I didn't even need to think about it.

Union with Christ is what most makes sense of the Christian life for me. Understanding what it was to be in Adam stops me from letting myself off the hook when I discover just how deep some particular sin might run in my heart. It might feel "natural" to me, but the Bible's teaching about what has happened to us in Adam is enough to show me that we all have a deeply unnatural sense of what is natural.

Union with Christ has been the game changer in my pursuit of holiness. Rather than seeing obedience to God as science-fiction-level unattainability, I see it as the proper outworking of who I really am in Jesus. Not that it's automatic and doesn't require all kinds of daily battles and bloodshed, but knowing that holiness is so thoroughly going with the grain of what is deepest in me gives daily energy and confidence. Sin might at times, sadly, be what I *want*, but it will never more be who I *am*. Those days are as far gone as Jesus's grave is empty, so unless he quits heaven and climbs back into it, I have every reason to look sin in the eye and know it's not ultimately going to win. It can talk a good game, but it doesn't have the power it once did.

Union with Christ is what helps me look to the future without fear. I am at the age when the warranty on my body has evidently expired, and it's not just my eyes that are a problem; my back and sciatic nerve have been making me look as though I'm moving around in slow motion. And while it's not as if nothing can be done to improve those problems (do your stretches, Allberry), it nevertheless augurs what is increasingly to come in the next couple of decades or so. But this doesn't have to bother me. I'm united to a Christ who is risen, bodily. My own physical resurrection is as sure as his own.

Union with Christ has buttressed my assurance. God really has justified me and done so justly. The bridegroom has shared all he has with the bride he is united to, and so we can be assured that God has forgiven us in a way that upholds his good, just character.

But perhaps more than anything else, union with Christ has fulfilled the deepest longings of my heart. Ever since I can remember, I have always longed for a deep friend to walk through life with, who would be there for me, whom I could even hide behind when I needed to. At times it has been an agonizing yearning. In my teenage years, a painful season of being bullied poured gasoline all over it, and I began to experience this longing as a debilitating anxiety. Who would there be to stand by me? What friend could ever be enough for me? Our souls are too heavy for any one of our friends to carry. Even the best human relationships can't be all that we need. But one has come who truly is all we need—a friend who is able to say, "I am with you *always*," without any hint of hyperbole. Being one with us, how could he not be? More than that, he embodies every perfection we most long for and need in a friend, and we can literally envelop ourselves in him, hide ourselves in him, console ourselves in him. We will never be too much for him, and he will never not be enough for us. What my heart has longed for all my life—in goofy ways, in sinful ways, in harmful ways, in confused ways—is all truly present in Jesus.

We have it all when we have him because he not only has it all but is all in all.

So whatever else might be true of me in this world, whatever else I might one day find myself to be in—in love, in debt, or (like Paul) in prison—nothing can take away from the surest reality: being in Christ.

Acknowledgments

ONE OF THE SWEETEST BLESSINGS of being in Christ—being in him together with other believers—was apparent throughout this whole project. I didn't do this on my own and couldn't have.

First, there were the theological giants whose own work on this glorious topic helped open my own eyes: Robert Letham, Michael Reeves, Glen Scrivener, Rory Shiner, Edward Donnelly.

Second, there are those whom God has so kindly surrounded me with here at Immanuel Nashville. T. J. Tims was always a brain on hand to pick, Ray Ortlund a further brain to pick when I wasn't sure T. J.'s was big enough. Ethan Kiteck was a sounding board on several occasions when I just needed someone to verbalize my thought process with. A very special word of thanks goes to Wade Urig, who read much of this book in its early (= terrible) draft and was a relentless encouragement when I was tempted to give up. A doctrine like this deserves a far more beautiful book than the one I've written, but Wade helped persuade me to keep writing anyway. Thank you, Wade.

Third, various churches have endured my teaching on this doctrine, which has greatly helped me sharpen my thinking and communication. I first taught on this topic at the weekend away for some of the congregations of St. Mary's Anglican Cathedral in Kuala Lumpur, Malaysia, in 2012; then at weekends for St. Ebbe's Oxford, UK, in 2013 and St. Nicholas Sevenoaks, UK, in 2016; and at my own church during that time, St. Mary's Maidenhead.

Fourth, it is always a privilege to work with a publisher as venerable and proficient as Crossway. Particular thanks must go to David Barshinger, who edited the book with forensic care, so that it is no longer littered with grammatical embarrassments, and made sure this British author didn't sound *too* British.

Virtually this whole book was written in the margins of time, much on planes when traveling (thanks, American Airlines), a few chapters while on vacation (thanks, Chuck, Hannah, and Gabe), and some in the home of Brian and Leslie Roe—along with Daniel, Sarah, and the wonderful newest addition, Ned— in Shincliffe, County Durham, UK. As always, their home is a beautiful place to write and think. Brian and Leslie, more than anyone else I know, have facilitated, blessed, and encouraged my writing over many years. This book is gratefully dedicated to them, with love.

General Index

abomination, 60
abortion, 55
abuse, 117
action movies, 80
Adam
    being "in," 52–56, 158
    as representative, 43–48
    as type of Christ, 48–49
adoption, 25, 33, 93
age to come, 98
Ananias, 10
Andrews, Thomas, 146
Andronicus, 11–12
apartheid, 127
apostles, 121, 128
Aquila, 12
armor of Christ, 110
assurance, 52, 58, 72–74, 154, 159
atheism, 58–59
atonement, 58, 59
authority, 87

baptism, 83
bearing, 131
bed-and-breakfast, 147
believers, 10–12, 53, 79
belonging, 2, 78
belt of truth, 110
Bieber, Justin, 67
biological sex, 126

biology, 100
blameworthiness, 32
blessings
    as abounding, 25–26
    to God, 26–29
    as spiritual, 30–35
    through union with Christ, 35–37
boasting, 71
bodies, as members of Christ, 102–3
body, 17–18
bonsai tree, 143–44
"born again," 14–15
branches, 16–17, 138, 145
Braveheart (film), 40
bridegroom, 64–65
briefcase drop, 62–63
Broadchurch (TV series), 28
brothers and sisters, 115

Calvin, John, 36
Cambodia, 98
Caribbean, 57
Carson, D. A., 137, 147n3
caste system, 127
celebration, 29, 65
character, 143
children, 46, 56
children of God, 94
chosen, 31–33
Christian (label), 7

Scripture Index

Also Available from Sam Allberry

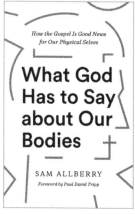

For more information, visit **crossway.org**.